HISTORY OF THE ROYAL AIR FORCE

MICHAEL SHARPE

p

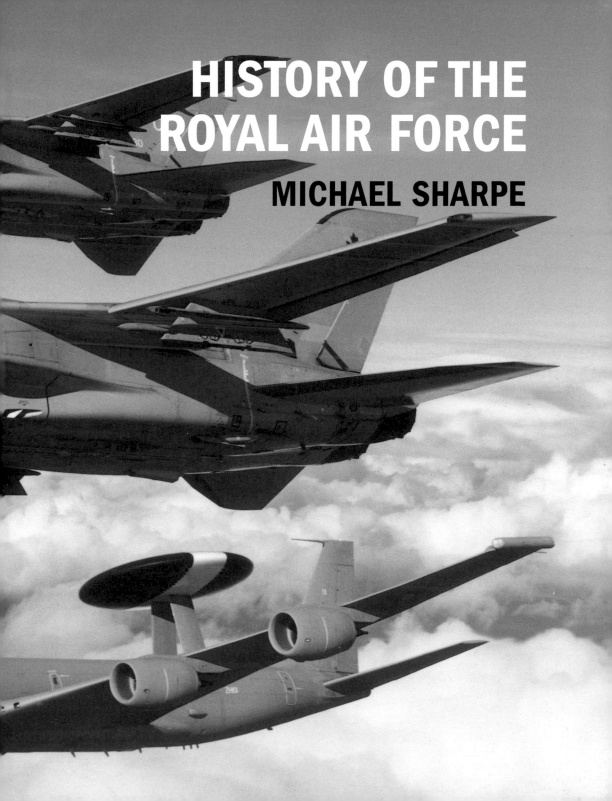

HISTORY OF THE
ROYAL AIR FORCE

MICHAEL SHARPE

This is a Parragon Book
This edition published in 2002
Parragon
Queen Street House
4 Queen Street
Bath BA1 1HE, UK

ISBN 0-75257-987-8

Editorial and design by
Amber Books Ltd
Bradley's Close
74–77 White Lion Street
London N1 9PF

Design: Jeremy Williams

Printed in Spain

Picture Acknowledgments
Boeing, British Aerospace, Dasa, Imperial War Museum,
Ministry of Defence, E. Nevill, Royal Air Force Museum,
TRH Pictures, US Army, Vickers and R. Winslade

Artwork Acknowledgements
All artworks: Aerospace Publishing

CONTENTS

INTRODUCTION

The end of the 20th century seems an appropriate time to reflect on 82 years of Royal Air Force history. The 60th anniversary of the Battle of Britain, the most famous chapter in RAF history, was commemorated in September 2000. The successful defence of mainland Britain in the second year of World War II, and its role in saving the country from Nazi invasion, elevated the importance of the RAF in the eyes of the British people and inspired in them a lasting debt of gratitude. Today, the event is rightly remembered as a defining moment in both British and world history.

Less well publicised, however, are the many other theatres of conflict in which the Service has been committed during peacetime. It is hoped, therefore, that this book will provide an insight into the less well-known aspects of RAF operations as well as their more famous exploits. The opening chapter looks at the growth of the Royal Flying Corps during World War I and its consolidation into the Royal Air Force, together with the Royal Naval Air Service, in April 1918.

The book then looks progressively at the RAFs struggle for survival in the inter-war years, the titanic battles of World War II, post-war austerity and the retreat from empire, the tense nuclear drama of the Cold War, and the Gulf War of 1991. In conclusion, it looks at the future of the RAF as we enter the new millennium.

Through their actions in peacetime and war the men and women of the Royal Air Force have established an enduring reputation for professionalism and courage, often in the face of extreme adversity. As the service faces the challenges of the new, it will carry that tradition into the next millennium.

FOUNDATIONS

Interest in aviation among the British military grew steadily, if undramatically, in the decade preceding World War I. Tethered helium-filled observation balloons made a useful contribution to British Army operations in South Africa during the Boer War of 1899–1902, carrying men aloft to plot the fall of artillery fire. After Orville and Wilbur Wright successfully flew the first heavier-than-air machine in 1903, the Imperial General Staff felt aircraft could make a contribution in this role, if only a limited one. However, reactionary cavalrymen and battleship admirals within the ranks remained highly sceptical of the flimsy and temperamental aircraft then available. Tentative steps were taken by forward-thinking officers in both the Army and the Royal Navy to exploit aircraft for military purposes, but they were hampered by limited resources and a lack of official interest.

In marked contrast, there was great enthusiasm among members of the public for the daring feats of Edwardian aeronauts. Many were doubtless driven by a rather ghoulish fascination with the dangers of the sport, but a few more prescient and enterprising individuals began to seek military backing for their experimental work. Among them was the pioneer aviator Samuel F Cody, who in October 1908 demonstrated the British Army Aeroplane No 1 to a gathering of military dignitaries at Farnborough in Hampshire.

A ROYAL FLYING CORPS

By 1910, the British Army was able to boast an air battalion within its Royal Regiment of Engineers, and the same year

BELOW: Avro York transport aircraft of the RAF en route to Berlin during the airlift of 1948–49. Less than three years after World War II ended, the RAF was carrying food, not bombs, to Berlin.

ROYAL AIRCRAFT FACTORY BE2C

The BE2c formed the backbone of RFC squadrons at the outbreak of World War I. The designation BE is an abbreviation of Blériot Experimental, but this refers to the type of design (a two-seater bi-plane with a tractor engine) rather than any involvement by the pioneering French aviator. Much of the design was the work of Geoffrey de Havilland, a Royal Aircraft Factory engineer who used the earlier BE1 as his starting point. The BE2 has the distinction of being the first British machine specifically intended for a military role, that of artillery spotting and reconnaissance. The BE2 was therefore designed to be stable, a feature that made it an exceptional photographic platform. The BE2c was a development of the basic design with lateral controls, as opposed to wing warping controls. This represented a considerable advance and ensured the aircraft remained in service with the RFC for the duration of the War. The Renault V8 water-cooled engine produced a maximum of 70-hp, sufficient to propel the BE2c to 130 km/h (82 mph). Endurance was in the region of 3.5 hours.

saw the foundation of a school of military flying at Eastchurch in Kent. The expansion of military aviation became the subject of a review by a sub-committee of the Imperial Defence Committee, which drafted a series of proposals for government approval. These included the establishment of a British military aeronautical service comprising a Military and a Naval Wing, a Central Flying School to train military pilots and the creation of the Royal Aircraft Factory at Farnborough, Berkshire for research and experimentation. A Royal Warrant issued by King George V on April 13, 1912, authorised the name of the new force as The Royal Flying Corps, which absorbed the air battalion of the Royal Engineers. Regulations, that arbiter of fear and abhorrence among the rank-and-file Tommies, were soon laid down for the new service.

PER ARDUA AD ASTRA

The famous motto of the RAF, which translates roughly from the Latin as Through Bolts and Bars to the Stars, was adopted from the esteemed Mulvany family of Ireland at the suggestion of a Royal Engineers officer. Nevertheless, a grand-sounding Latin motto and a Royal Warrant could not detract from the fact that when Captain Frederick H Sykes, late of the 15th (the Kings) Hussars, came to take up his appointment as commander of the new unit he had barely four aircraft at his disposal. A further problem was that the two wings of the RFC were administered separately, by the War Office and the Admiralty.

Two years after the creation of the Royal Flying Corps, the only tangible link between the two Wings was the Central

Flying School. The Navy favoured its own flying school and there was little similarity in working practices, or joint doctrine, with the Army.

At this time, the Royal Navy was the most powerful maritime force in the world and was undoubtedly the senior British military service, with much influence in Parliament. The Lords of the Admiralty actively opposed inter-service links and in June 1914 the RFC was forced to cede the Naval Wing to the Royal Navy. The Admiralty renamed it the Royal Naval Air Service on July 1, just in case there were any doubts as to who was in charge.

It was to the Admiraltys credit, however, that they considered the aircraft as a weapon of attack long before their Army counterparts, and from very early on promoted its development for offensive operations, particularly against the German submarine and Zeppelin threat. Bombsights were designed for naval aircraft and perfected during trials, and in July 1914 a Short seaplane made the first successful ascent carrying a torpedo. Airborne wireless sets were developed, vastly improving surface-to-air communications.

THE PATH TO WAR

The balloons and kites of No 1 Squadron, RFC, were transferred to the RNAS in January 1914 and by the outbreak of World War I on August 4, the RNAS had grown to a strength of 128 officers and 700 ratings, operating seven airships and about 70 aircraft of varying quality. No 1 Squadron subsequently reequipped with heavier-than-air machines. Following the creation of Nos 2 and 3 squadrons in 1912, three further RFC squadrons were authorised by Parliament. They were equipped with aircraft built predominantly by the Royal Aircraft Factory, which relied heavily on RE (Reconnaissance Experimental), FE (Farman Experimental), or BE (Blériot Experimental) bi-plane designs. The most important of them was the BE2c, of which more is said elsewhere.

In early 1914, the main role of the RFC was considered to be artillery observation. Stability was the governing factor in the design of military aircraft, and this was to be found in a staggered bi-wing configuration. Monoplanes were faster, more manoeuvrable and more difficult to control, and were considered dangerous in all but the most experienced hands.

In early July 1914, with the War imminent, the RFC decamped en masse to Netheravon in Wiltshire for a period of intense training, with the aim of maximising the proficiency of its personnel in military air operations. World War I erupted four weeks later. Nos 2 and 3 Squadrons joined the British Expeditionary Force in France on August 13, followed later by Nos 4 and 5. There was much ill-informed talk that the war would be over by Christmas, but in the event, it dragged on for four harrowing years. It was the first conflict in which military air power played a major role, and the one that eventually spawned the Royal Air Force.

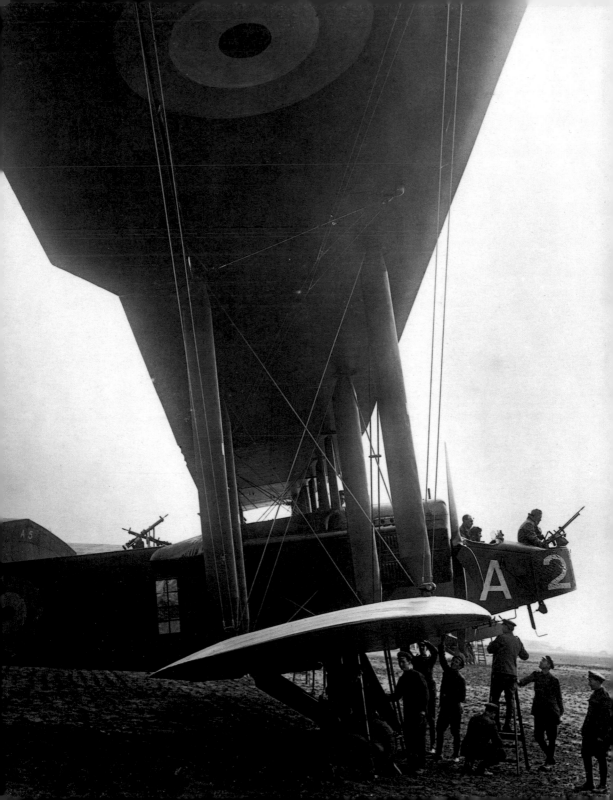

CHAPTER 1

INTO BATTLE

In 1914 war finally erupted in France and British military aviation faced its first major test in combat. So successful did the RFC and RNAS prove that during the four years of war they were expanded out of all proportion and, in April 1918, united to form the Royal Air Force.

World War I witnessed a revolution in British military aviation. In less than four years of war, the four squadrons and 860 personnel of the Royal Flying Corps expanded to 385 squadrons and nearly 293,000 personnel. The conflict also acted as a proving ground for the role aircraft would play in future warfare. Although there is little doubt that the outcome of the war was decided by the artillery and infantry,

ABOVE: An early propaganda photograph in which an airman demonstrates the crude way in which early aerial bombs were aimed and delivered.

LEFT: Groundcrew prepare a Handley Page 0/400 heavy bomber for flight. The 0/400 was designed to provide the RAF with an aircraft with sufficient range to attack Germany from Britain.

and that the aeroplane played only a supporting role, the impact of its arrival on the battlefield can be gauged from a government report of June 1917, which concluded that aircraft would revolutionise future warfare and render conventional forces obsolete. In April 1918, seven months before the end of the War, control of the national air forces was finally wrested from the War Office and the Admiralty, so paving the way for the inauguration of the independent Royal Air Force.

EYES OVER THE FRONT

By the summer of 1914, aircraft had become an accepted part of military planning, but the range of roles the RFC could undertake was limited by the performance of the aircraft it operated. At the outbreak of war, four squadrons of the RFC

ABOVE: The practice of clearing flying clothes of anything but essential items before patrol prevented information that could be of any military significance from falling into enemy hands.

were sent to France with the British Expeditionary Force to undertake aerial reconnaissance for the army. In France, the RFC could draw on 63 aircraft and 95 transport vehicles, operated by 105 officers and 755 men. The aircraft were an assortment of Blériot monoplanes, BE2s, Farmans, Avros and BE8s. The widely varying capabilities of British aircraft types were not deemed a cause for concern, as neither formation flying nor coordinated air tactics had yet been developed. Nor was fitted armament, although many pilots and observers took personal arms for use should they be forced down in enemy territory. The French Aéronautique Militaire was the best equipped effective air force at the time, with 132 front line machines and as many again held in reserve. Opposing the Anglo-French alliance, the Germany Army Air Service had more machines, but these were mainly poor copies of French designs and there were fewer pilots available to fly them.

In the first weeks of the War, when the manoeuvrings of the ground forces were relatively fluid, RFC aircrew were utilised as the eyes of the army, much as had been expected, flying reconnaissance missions to observe the enemy during the British retreat. These missions soon proved their worth and were the source of much useful intelligence. Attempts by the German Army under General Alexander von Kluck to outflank the British were detected from the air, enabling the BEF commander, Sir John French, to escape the trap and earning glowing praise for the RFC. The deployment of most

---

COMMUNIQUE NO 27 COVERING THE PERIOD 30 SEPTEMBER TO OCTOBER 6, 1918

During the period under review we have claimed officially 86 E.A (Enemy aircraft) brought down and 27 driven out of control. In addition, I E.A was brought down by A.A. Fifty-six of our machines are missing. Approximately 223 tons of bombs were dropped and 4,953 plates (photographic) exposed.

of the RFC strength to France, however, left precious few reserves on which to draw, and left little capacity for air defence against the feared Zeppelin airships.

FIRST EXCHANGES

As the German attack became bogged down in the mud of northern France, the task of aerial reconnaissance was supplemented by the need for artillery spotting. Air-to-ground communications were limited, with few wireless sets available. However, when combined with effective aerial photography, it was possible to improve the accuracy of artillery fire. In November, the RFC field units were more effectively organised into Wings, each of two squadrons, one of which was attached to each of the two armies of the BEF. A further three squadrons were attached to the RFC headquarters at St Omer. Aircraft could now be concentrated at points where they were most needed, rather than scattered along the whole front, enabling other squadrons to focus on the work of supporting ground units.

Aerial bombardment, of course, was still in its infancy. Strategic bombing was no more than a theory dreamed up in academies of military science. Those who envisaged mass bombing raids against foreign cities had only to look at the tiny, flimsy-looking aircraft then available to realise that such a capability was some way off. Some rudimentary exercises in bombing had been carried out prior to the war, but over the Western front in the autumn of 1914, these usually amounted to nothing more than dropping hand grenades onto enemy lines.

The RNAS, which deployed to the Dunkirk area on 26 August, was rather more offensively minded. Naval pilots attacked the Zeppelin sheds at Dusseldorf and Friedrichshaven on separate occasions during the autumn, destroying one airship at the former base and causing damage at both. Large numbers of aircraft were subsequently diverted to defend the sheds, which may be seen as an important development in the strategy of aerial warfare. Although bombing missions were occasionally carried out by the RFC against known targets, such as railway marshalling yards and transportation centres, notably during the Battle of Neuve Chappelle in July 1915, strategic bombing, however, was a much later development.

The main tasks of RFC squadrons during the first year of conflict were long-range reconnaissance, short-range photo-reconnaissance, and artillery observation. It was the increasing effectiveness of aircraft in these roles that spurred the development of air-to-air combat techniques during late 1915 and early 1916.

Even without the concerted attentions of hostile aircraft, RFC pilots faced many dangers. The vagaries of the north European weather could severely hinder air operations and only served to highlight the general frailty of the aircraft and their limited performance. This situation was only slightly improved as better aircraft became available. Night flying was something that happened by accident rather than choice. Friendly fire incidents were common. Pilots on both sides of the line were frequently shot at by their own troops, most of

Captain Albert Ball, No 56 Squadron, RFC France 1917. Captain Ball is holding the propeller spinner of the Nieuport 17 scout that he flew rather than the SE5 favoured by his squadron. He is wearing the field service dress of a Royal Flying Corps officer, which included breeches and high boots. The badge of the RFC is on his cap and lapel, and the badges of his rank are on his sleeve.

whom had, quite understandably, not troubled to learn the differences between a Fokker and a Farman. In October 1914, RFC squadrons received an order to paint the undersides of their aircraft wings with a Union Jack to help identification. When it was found that the central cross was easily confused with the German Iron Cross from the ground, the familiar vermilion, white and ultramarine Type A(i) roundel (a reversal of the French blue, white and red marking) was hastily substituted. This remained in use until 1942. The RNAS used a red ring from December 1914, but adopted the RFC pattern roundel from November of the next year.

FIGHTER SQUADRONS

Warplanes designed for air-to-air combat did not exist in 1914. As the fighting stagnated on the Western Front, however, the opposing air forces found themselves competing for the same airspace. Encounters with enemy airmen became more common, but a coherent strategy for fighting aircraft had not yet emerged. Hostile exchanges in the air sometimes amounted to no more than a shake of the fist and a volley of curses! When they realised that slow, lumbering German reconnaissance machines offered an easy target, some enthusiastic RFC pilots had their aircraft fitted with machine guns,

BELOW: Hugh Trenchard, whose singleminded determination, from the time of his appointment as chief of staff in 1918 through the postwar years, effectively created the RAF.

HUGH TRENCHARD

The man who is widely regarded as the Father of the Royal Air Force was a regular army officer, though a trained pilot, before he transferred to the RFC in 1913. In August 1915, he was appointed the RFC field commander in France. Trenchard's faith in aerial warfare was based primarily on the development of strategic bombing aircraft, and his preliminary appointment as chief of staff to the RAF in January 1918 reflected the government's commitment to the concept.

Unhappy as an administrator, he resigned in April and took up command of the Independent Air Force. Trenchard continued to pursue the development of the RAF as a strategic force in the postwar years, and also laid the foundations for many of its most famous institutions. He was a bombastic and forceful man, but well liked and respected by his men, and was a driving force behind the creation of an independent air service.

---

but more casualties occurred because of accidents, rather than through combat.

In the autumn of 1915, this situation began to change. More effective air-to-air combat became possible as new and better aircraft became available. The most important of these was the Fokker monoplane introduced into service by the German Army Air Service. The Fokker was not in itself an outstanding aircraft, but had been designed by Dutchman Anthony Fokker with a interrupter mechanism to allow the machine-gun to fire through the arc of the propeller. The clear advantages of this system over a pivoting nose-mounted machine gun or fixed upper wing-mounted machine gun are evident.

Another important development helped the Imperial German Army Air Service to gain an early lead in aerial combat. Until the spring of 1915, the Germans had operated a mixture of aircraft types within squadrons that were expected to carry out any mission assigned to them. Standardisation of aircraft within the Fliegerabteilungen (flying units) became possible because of the large numbers of aircraft ordered from German factories. In August 1915, seven single-role German fighter squadrons were formed. Two of the squadron commanders, Oswald Boelcke and Max Immelman, took advantage of the standardisation within their units to evolve tactics involving close-formation flying, and later, the use of large formations based on mutually supporting pairs. The tactics Boelcke fostered helped to assert German air superiority over the Western front in the autumn of 1915 and were the cause of significant RFC losses. They still form the basis of air combat techniques today.

The RFC had no interrupter mechanism at this time and was forced to rely on pusher-engined aircraft with observer/gunner in the nose, or tractor machines with armament mounted over the wing. The British were equally slow to organise specific fighter units. The first squadron equipped with the two-seat Vickers FB5 Gunbus an , designed from the outset for fighting duties, did not arrive in France until the summer of 1915. This coincided with the replacement of Major-General Sir David Henderson as commander of the RFC by Major-General Sir Hugh Trenchard.

NEW AIRCRAFT

A new and crucial change in air warfare came in 1916 with the arrival of fresh aircraft types, which offered improved performance, and much more importantly, reliability. Improvements in aircraft performance were found by increasing engine power, since it was not feasible to reduce the weight of these already flimsy aircraft to increase aerodynamic efficiency. In 1914, 80 percent of military aircraft were powered by a derivative of the rotary engine installed in the 25-hp monoplane that had carried Louis Blériot across the English Channel in 1909. This engine had the advantage of a high power-to-weight ratio, but like all rotary engines, it also suffered numerous shortcomings.

A major problem was the fact that a tremendous amount of torque was created by the engine cylinders, which revolved around the central crankshaft. This caused considerable handling problems. It soon became clear to aircraft manufacturers that the more powerful stationary radial, in-line or V-engines provided the key to superior aircraft. By the end of World War I in 1918, the horsepower that was available from engines such as these had quadrupled, increasing aircraft performance twice over.

No 24 Squadron was the first in the RFC to be equipped with a single-seat fighter, the de Havilland DH2. The squadron arrived in France in February 1916, and, although tricky to fly, this aircraft brought an end to the superiority enjoyed by the Fokker E-series and helped establish air superiority over the Somme in July. German fighter development continued apace, with the Albatros C-series and the Halberstadt, which effectively rendered the DH2 obsolete, but the aircraft remained in service until well into 1917.

In April 1916, service deliveries began of the Sopwith 1 1/2 Strutter (so named because of the arrangement of struts attaching the upper wing), one of the most important RFC aircraft of the War. It was the first aircraft to be designed from the outset with a synchronised gun firing through the propeller arc. By the end of the War some 1,513 had been delivered. The Strutter is a classic design whose basic layout formed the pattern for most subsequent RFC aircraft. Not least among these was the single-seat Sopwith Scout or Pup, which entered service later in the year. Production of the Pup totalled over 5,000, giving some indication of the extent to which military aviation was expanding at this time. The Pup was the first in a new class of British aircraft – the fighting scout. Once forward armament had been mastered by both sides, a series of small, single-seat designs emerged – the Albatros D-types, Sopwith Triplane, Fokker D-VIII, Spad S-types, and the Sopwith Camel among them – and brought fame to that most dashing breed of airman, the ace.

BELOW: A squadron of SE-5s run-up their engines prior to a patrol. The registration letters on the aircraft in the foreground have been scratched out by the wartime censor.

DE HAVILLAND DH2

The DH2 was the first single-seat fighter in RAF service. It was introduced during a crucial period of the air war and helped to counter the Fokker scourge over the Western Front. It was designed as a pusher by Geoffrey de Havilland in order to get around the problem of fitting a machine gun, because at this time the British had no interrupter or synchronising gear. The Lewis .303 machine gun was manually aimed by the pilot with one hand while he flew the aircraft with the other. Although tricky to fly, the DH2 was very manoeuvrable when competently handled. For its day, it had adequate performance, though the Monosoupape (single valve) Gnome engine tended to blow its cylinders off whilst running. Altogether, 450 of these aircraft were built, about 300 serving in France and the rest in the Middle East.

By July 1916, RFC strength had grown to 31 squadrons, with 410 aircraft and 426 pilots. The air battle over the Somme lasted until November of that year and cost 308 killed, wounded or missing.

In December, the RFC was authorised to raise 106 service squadrons, with 95 to be held in reserve. Expansion on this scale called for restructuring in the aircraft industry. In 1914, British aircraft production was little more than a cottage industry, with annual output measured in tens rather than hundreds of machines. In 1916, this figure rose to 1,782, but this was still a fraction of the 7,320 machines produced in the period between January and October 1918. However, the vast majority of machines produced during 1916 were of already obsolescent design. Few Sopwith Pups were available to the RFC, and the emergence of superior German aircraft later in the year figured greatly in the devastating losses suffered by the RFC in the spring of 1917.

BLOODY APRIL

The combat superiority of the new Jagdstaffeln (German fighter units) had been amply demonstrated during the latter stages of the Somme offensive of 1916, but no new Allied aircraft had emerged to counter their Albatros fighters by spring of the next year. In planning the spring offensive at Arras, it was felt that the 3-1 numerical advantage enjoyed by Allied aircraft could compensate for obsolete machines such as the BE2 and RE8 and enable the RFC to perform intensive army cooperation duties. In preparation for the ground attack, the RFC launched an air offensive against German airfields, following this with reconnaissance and artillery spotting missions. The aim was to draw the Germans

RIGHT: A youthful-looking Captain Albert Ball, winner of the Victoria Cross and one of the first British heroes of the air.

away from the front and allow the observation aircraft free rein, but the cost proved appallingly high. In the event, 361 aircrew and over 300 aircraft were lost during April alone. The average life expectancy of an RFC pilot fell to 23 days, before the arrival of large numbers of more capable aircraft during May began to redress the balance.

Losses like these would have been unsustainable were it not for a concerted campaign to recruit pilots from both civilian life and the other services. The number of pilots under training rose to 1,300 a month, but it should be remembered that their flying course amounted to only 17–18 hours. The real problem for the Corps, however, was a lack of skilled technicians to maintain the aircraft. Something like 47 ground staff were needed to keep each aircraft in the air, and training schemes could not keep pace with the rate of expansion. In June 1917, it was decided that, to redress the balance, the training of mechanics would be consolidated at Halton Park. This establishment became one of the cornerstones of the RAF. Another feature of this period was the establishment of the Women's Royal Air Force, created with volunteers from women's auxiliary units.

DOGFIGHTS

The month of April also saw the advent of the first mass dogfights. The term was extended to mean any combat between two aircraft, yet most experts acknowledge that the first true dogfight took place over Flanders on April 24, 1917 involving some 50 German scouts and 44 RFC machines. The

*RIGHT: **Major Edward "Mick" Mannock, who was the highest scoring British pilot of the war with 73 victories. He was shot down in April 1918 by ground fire.***

arrival of more capable aircraft during mid-1917 gave the Allied air forces an advantage they never lost again, helped in no small measure by chronic shortages within the German aircraft manufacturing industry. In these aerial battles, heroes were made out of ordinary men.

THE ACES

The dangers of aerial combat held a special attraction for the public, and a popular cult was established during 1916 around the exploits of high-scoring pilots. The press in their respective countries were always eager to capitalise on the exploits of French ace Georges Guynemer, the German pilots Oswald Boelcke, Max Immelman, Baron Manfred von Richtofen, Ernst Udet, and Hermann Göring, and the American Eddie Rickenbacker, encouraged in no small part by government propagandists. The RFC were slightly more reluctant to glamorise individuals, realising that resentment could easily be fostered among pilots with less high-profiles but equally dangerous duties. Albert Ball, Edward "Mick" Mannock, Billy Bishop and James McCudden were well known within the service, but their identities and exploits never received the popular acclaim of Boelcke, Immelman or Richtofen. The reality, however, was often far removed from the glamour. Casualties were enormously high on both sides; few new recruits to fighter squadrons could expect their war to last more than two-and-a-half months. Parachutes were never issued in the RFC, even though they were available, as senior officers were convinced that it would encourage British pilots to jump prematurely. Requests for their use were regarded as tantamount to cowardice. In retrospect, it would have been much wiser to enforce their use. Such a policy may well have saved many lives.

THE ZEPPELIN THREAT

Zeppelin attacks on the Britain had taken place as early as December 1914, and continuing raids during early 1915 placed the onus for the mainland defence on the RFC. The physical impact of these raids was modest, but their psychological effect on the British public was powerful enough to warrant the deployment of the RFC on home defence duties. These units were initially equipped with obsolete aircraft such as the BE2c and by December 1916, there were 12 squadrons ranged against the airships. The German Army Air Service also developed long-range bomber aircraft; the best of them were the Gotha series and the giant Zeppelin-Staaken R-Types. The first raid, by a solitary Gotha, took place on November 28, 1916. The scale of the raids was steadily increased until June 13 the following year, when 14 Goths GIVs bombed London in broad daylight, killing 162 people. The boldness of this attack came as a profound shock

to the whole country. The RFC could find no ready answer to the bomber threat, which continued until August 1918. High-flying airships and bombers were difficult to intercept, even with fighters which, in all truth, could have been better employed elsewhere.

THE INDEPENDENT BOMBING FORCE

The RFC possessed no long-range bombing capability at the start of the war, and only with the development of the twin-engined Handley Page 0/100 and 0/400 were they able to mount effective strategic attacks on German industry. The energetic RFC commander, Trenchard, was appointed to head the RAF in April 1918 but felt unable to work with the new Secretary of State for Air, Harold Harmsworth, Viscount Rothermere. Trenchard was thus charged with overseeing the creation of the new Independent Bombing Force being set up in France. The General Staff had grand visions for this force. In the spring of 1918 the war against Germany had very definitely turned in favour of the Allies, but was by no means won, and it was planned to raise upwards of 100 squadrons to drive the Germans to the bargaining table. In the event, only 15 squadrons were raised, but from June 1918 the force carried out 162 raids and dropped some 350,000 tons of bombs, though in the face of mounting losses to anti-aircraft fire.

WAR AT SEA

Mention must be made of the activities of the RNAS, who were later to form one of the two constituent elements of the

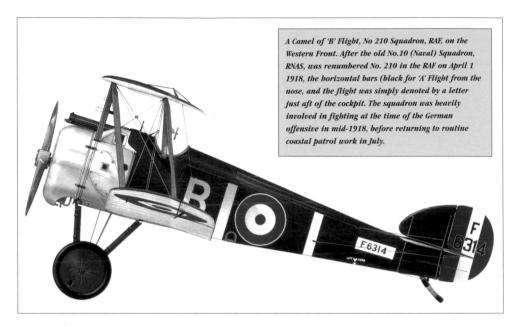

A Camel of 'B' Flight, No 210 Squadron, RAF, on the Western Front. After the old No.10 (Naval) Squadron, RNAS, was renumbered No. 210 in the RAF on April 1 1918, the horizontal bars (black for 'A' Flight from the nose, and the flight was simply denoted by a letter just aft of the cockpit. The squadron was heavily involved in fighting at the time of the German offensive in mid-1918, before returning to routine coastal patrol work in July.

RAF. In addition to the crucial twin roles of maritime reconnaissance and spotting, the airships and flying boats of the RNAS were tasked with patrolling for a new and threatening weapon, the U-boat. The long duration of airships made them ideal for this role, as the German U-boat of this period could remain submerged for only 60–80 miles. Some 200 were built during the War, operating mainly from bases in East Anglia. In addition to the airships, seaplanes such as the Felixstowe F2A, the forerunner of a famous series of RAF flying boats, proved a useful counter to the U-boat scourge. Bombs and guns gave their crews an offensive capacity. Of even greater importance was the ability to force the submarine crew to dive for shelter under the waves, where they were less of a threat. However, airship operations were often hindered by bad weather, and seaplanes could not rove with impunity. The obvious solution was to deploy aircraft on ships. A Short biplane had flown from the specially modified battleship HMS Africa in 1912 and during the course of the War, HMS Furious was modified during construction to carry a complement of three seaplanes and five Sopwith Pup landplanes. When the decision was taken to amalgamate the RNAS into the new RAF, the four fleet carriers remained under naval control.

CREATION OF THE ROYAL AIR FORCE

In the early part of the War, separate control of the air squadrons had worked satisfactorily, but as the air war developed – particularly during the temporary phases of enemy air superiority, such as the domination of the Fokkers

in the winter of 1915–16, and the daylight raids on England in 1917 – shortcomings became apparent. As a result, there was prolonged public controversy about Britain's whole air organisation. In June 1917 a Cabinet Committee was formed under General Jan Christiaan Smuts, the South African soldier and statesman, to examine the future of the air arm. Its first report was completed by July and recommended that a single command be established for all fighter aircraft in Britain, all the anti-aircraft and searchlight batteries, and all the observation posts.

In October, a further report was ready. It contained far more radical recommendations and ones that were widely opposed among the General Staff. Smuts foresaw a future where aerial operations would be the most important aspect of warfare, and believed that a separate Air Ministry should be established. He observed: "The day may not be far off when aerial operations with their devastation of enemy lands and destruction of industries and populous centres on a vast scale may become the principal operations of the war, to which older forms of military and naval operations may become secondary and subordinate."

In retrospect, Smuts foresight is all too clear, yet the report was not well received, neither by the Admiralty nor the War Office. Many senior officers, Haig among them, opposed the very idea of a separate air force, while others thought that the middle of a desperate war was no time for such an upheaval. Nonetheless, acting on Smuts recommendations in this and another report published in October, the government prepared The Air Force (Constitution) Act, which was passed on November 29, 1917. The merger of the RNAS and RFC took effect on April 1, 1918, effectively absorbing the 3,000 aircraft and 67,000 officers and ratings of the RNAS into the RAF.

PEACE

Allied domination over the Western Front was never challenged during the final months of the War. Underpinning this superiority was the fact that the German aircraft industry could not keep pace with the mounting losses. The intensity of bombing raids carried out by the Independent Bombing Force steadily increased, and a specialist night fighter squadron formed in France to engage German raiders. Communiqués from this period also show the increase in the range of activities undertaken by the RAF. Reconnaissance continued to be a priority, but strafing attacks on airfields and supply depots assumed great importance and continued until November 11, the last day of the War.

"September 30. Weather low clouds, heavy rainstorms. No night bombing was possible. 8 tons of bombs dropped by day. November 11. Weather fair but misty. 20 tonnes of bombsdropped by night and 3/4 tonne by day. No enemy aircraft activity. 214 Sqn carried out a successful raid on Louvain railway sidings and junction during the night, 50kg

BELOW: Pilots and Sopwith Camels of No 203 Squadron of the recently formed Royal Air Force at Izel Les Hameau in July 1918. Note the mixture of naval and army uniforms.

FROM: *SAGITTARIUS RISING* BY CECIL DAY LEWIS

"(Albert) Ball was a quiet, simple little man. His one relaxation was the violin and his favourite after-dinner amusement was to light a red magnesium flare outside his hut and walk round it in his pyjamas, fiddling! He was meticulous in the care for his machines, guns, and in the examination of his ammunition. He never flew for amusement. The only trips he took, apart from offensive air patrols, were the minimal requisite to test his engines or fire at the ground target sighting his guns. He never boasted or criticised, but his example was tremendous."

(112lb) bombs being dropped and many direct hits being obtained. An ammunition train was hit, causing explosions and fires all over the sidings. Hostilities ceased at 11.00."

The RAF ended World War I bearing little relation to either of the two services from which it had been formed. By December 1918 the RAF possessed more than 22,000 aircraft, making it easily the world's largest air force. The cost of victory had been high, though. Some 16,623 personnel were listed as casualties 6,166 of them aircrew. However, in the 20 years of peace that followed, the RAF was faced with another crisis that threatened to destroy it and left it ill-prepared for the second war with Germany.

CHAPTER 2

POLICING THE EMPIRE

In the large-scale defence cuts of the post-war years the Royal Air Force found justification for its existence in the role of colonial policeman. Many of the institutions of the RAF were established at this time, but a lack of effective funding for the Service left it poorly prepared for war in 1939.

As Britain struggled to recover from World War I, the RAF found its role in Europe diminished and its strength greatly reduced. During the two decades following the War, budgetary constraints and continued opposition to the notion of an independent air force meant that a series of crises in territories under British administration tested the RAFs ability to fulfil its expected role as a peace-keeping force.

ABOVE: Aircraft of the Royal Air Force, including Hawker Furies (front rank), and Gloster Gamecocks (second rank), mustered at Mildenhall for a Royal Review in the 1930s.

LEFT: An RAF recruiting poster. "Seeing the world" invariably meant a posting to the Middle East, where the RAF was most heavily committed during the inter-war years.

WHITE PAPER

In November 1919, Winston Churchill was appointed Secretary of State for War and Air. One of his first actions was to invite Hugh Trenchard, now Marshal of the Royal Air Force, to accept the post of Chief of the Air Staff. Trenchard realised that large scale defence spending would be an anathema to the public and, as few people cared to imagine another European war in their lifetime, they saw no need for a large RAF presence in Britain for air defence. He shrewdly judged that, while the ambitions of the service would have to be modest, there was a vital need to justify its existence during peacetime through positive action.

Trenchard drew up a White Paper for the future of the Service, entitled "An Outline of the Scheme for the Permanent Organisation of the Royal Air Force", dated

ABOVE: *A dramatic poster promoting the first Hendon airshow in 1920. The airshow became a massively popular annual event and did much for RAF public relations.*

December 11, 1919. The Paper was put before Parliament, which agreed to a very modest annual budget of £15 million pounds. In the document, Trenchard highlighted the need for quality and good economic management in the service. Perhaps the most important aspect of the paper, though, was the three pages devoted to "the extreme importance of training", in order to create a strong skill base among the future leaders of the service.

It was also suggested that RAF squadrons could play a vital role in policing the far-flung British Empire and act as a cost-effective replacement for expensive permanent garrisons. Air policing was a new and untested concept at this time, yet it emerged as the central role of the peacetime RAF and forms an important part of its history

THE MIDDLE EAST

At the Versailles Treaty of 1919, which ended the war with Germany, Britain was given a mandate to administer much of the Middle East, including some former colonies of the Ottoman Turkish Empire. The British government had a vested interest in maintaining stability in India and Egypt. India was regarded as the "jewel" of the British Empire and represented a enormous overseas investment. The Suez Canal, the vital route to India and the rest of Asia, passed through Egyptian territory. This was why Egypt was chosen as an ideal staging post for a semi-permanent RAF garrison, with the added bonus that it lay within easy reach of the most likely areas of unrest in the Middle East region.

The Royal Air Force was engaged in small scale disputes with tribesmen on the North-West Frontier of India in 1915, and in May 1919 more serious fighting erupted in the same region when the son of the hereditary ruler, the Amir Ammanullah, tried to rally his divided people by launching an invasion of India. In the four-week war two RAF squadrons, Nos 31 and 114, flew missions in direct support of the British Army and carried out extensive bombing raids against rebel strongholds. These culminated in the bombing of the Amir's palace in Kabul, the Afghan capital, an action which drove him to sue for peace. However, large numbers of Pathan warriors of the Mahsud and Waziri tribes refused to accept the peace and continued fighting and the RAF was ordered to mount air raids against them in November. After a month of daily assaults the RAF realised their enemy had become less passive and vulnerable to air attack. These suspicions were realised when three RAF aircraft were brought down by rifle fire during a raid against Pathan forces in the Ahnai Jangi Gorge on January 14, 1920. Eventually, a force of some 29,000 ground troops, supported by 34,000 non-combatants, was deployed to the region and succeeded in quashing the rebellion by early May of 1920. During these operations, the RAF flew many missions in support of the ground forces, and despite the enormous difficulties posed by the terrain and the hostile weather, acquitted itself well. In retrospect, the force of six squadrons was probably inadequate for the scale of the task.

SOMALILAND

Elsewhere during 1920, the RAF saw action in the colony of Somaliland, on the western coast of Africa. Hostilities against the occupying British forces had escalated during World War I, under the leadership of the tribal leader Sheikh Mohammed bin Abdullah Hassan, who took the title of sayyid (prince) but was known in the British press as the "Mad Mullah". Attempts by the Army to bring the sayyid to heel had failed, and with the prospect of another expensive expedition looming, the Colonial Secretary called on Trenchard to suggest a cheaper solution to the problem. Trenchard offered to employ RAF aircraft against the sayyid, supported by the modest ground forces already in the country. A small force of eight DH9 aircraft was shipped from Egypt to Berbera and became operational on January 21. In February, bombing attacks on the sayyid's camp forced him to flee to Abyssinia, were he died of influenza in 1921. The

THE AVRO 504

The Avro 504N formed the backbone of RAF training units from 1915 until 1933. Although originally designed as a reconnaissance and light bomber aircraft, it was a stable and forgiving machine and was soon adopted as a trainer. The 504N was powered by a 180-hp Armstrong Siddeley Lynx engine, providing a top speed of 160 km/h (100 mph) and an endurance of three hours.

Colonial Secretary reported happily that with estimated costs of only £77,000, the Somaliland affair had been the cheapest war in history.

MESOPOTAMIA

Financial constraints were a constant bugbear for the armed services in the austere environment of post-war Britain. Churchill, as Secretary of State for War and Air, had warned in August 1919 that a way would have to be found to reduce the costly garrison of 25,000 British and 80,000 Indian troops in Iraq. Air policing was once again perceived as the most cost-effective solution and Trenchard was duly asked if he would be prepared to "take Mesopotamia on", with the inducement of an extra £7 million added to the budget of the Royal Air Force. This plan drew heavy criticism from the two other services, who had determined to dismantle the Royal Air Force in the face of growing pressures on the Defence Budget. Trenchard saw it as a useful opportunity to establish an independent role for the Service and rapidly drew up a plan to station 10 of the 33 RAF squadrons in Mesopotamia. After a full scale uprising had broken out in the summer of 1920, this plan was rapidly put into practice, as a cheaper alternative to increasing the size of the army garrison.

Nevertheless, it was clear that aircraft alone would not be enough to carry out colonial policework, and the RAF was thus required to recruit a small army of supplementary ground troops, constituting locally raised troops, armoured car units, pack animals and nine battalions of British and Indian infantry. The command of these forces was given to Air Vice-Marshal John Maitland Salmond, who had replaced Trenchard in command of the RFC in 1918. Almost as soon as the RAF deployed to Iraq (as Mesopotamia became from 1922) it was required to provide a deterrent to Turkish incursions into the north of the country, which were aimed at reoccupying land taken from them at the Treaty of Versailles. By the autumn of 1922, a considerable force of seven squadrons, backed by the seaplane carrier HMS *Pegasus* and aircraft carrier HMS *Argus*, were ranged against the forces of the Turkish nationalist leader Kemal Ataturk. Their presence, and a hardline British diplomatic approach, proved sufficient to deter the Turks from attack.

Despite the difficulty of the conditions under which the RAF was forced to operate, with hopelessly insufficient logistical support at all stages, the action proved that the Service

*BELOW: **Pictured foreground during July 1919 is Air Vice-Marshal Sir John Maitland Salmond, mastermind of the successful and influential RAF operation in Mesopotamia in 1920–2.***

could move with admirable haste to any crisis area and operate under extreme pressures once in theatre.

Domestic unrest in northern Iraq occupied the RAF for the latter part of the 1920s. The most serious uprising involved several tribes in Kurdistan. led by the British-appointed Governor of the Sulaimania district, Sheik Mahmud. After learning of Mahmud's plan to attack the British stronghold of Kirkuk, an attack was launched on Sulaimania, his main town, forcing him to seek sanctuary in Persia (Iran). The operation to drive the rebel leader from Iraq involved close coordination between the airborne and ground forces of the RAF, and helped them to gain valuable experience in deterring the renewed attacks made by Mahmud in the summer of 1923. Although operations against Mahmud continued until 1931, the increased RAF strength in Iraq and its growing experience of the terrain dwindled the threat Mahmud represented to the stability of the region.

COLONIAL POLICEMEN

The RAF campaign in northern Iraq did much to bolster Trenchard's belief in the ability of the Service to operate as a colonial police force, and what was more, one which could

BELOW: A de Havilland DH9 in flight over Baghdad. With such aircraft the RAF fought a protracted campaign in Mesopotamia against insurgent elements.

VICKERS VERNON

This 12-seat passenger transport was the first RAF aircraft built specifically for carrying troops. Its design was based on the Vimy bomber of 1917, and the first Vernon joined No 45 Squadron at Hinaidi in 1922. It was not a machine remarkable for its performance; the two Napier Lion II engines gave the aircraft a cruising speed of only 130 km/h (80 mph) and it could carry its two crew and 12 passengers over a range of 500km (320 miles).

---

operate more quickly, effectively and cheaply than conventional forces. There is little doubt, however, that, in theatre, conditions were extraordinarily harsh for the RAF personnel. The climate was often intolerable, the boredom intense and the living conditions primitive. There were only limited medical facilities at the numerous RAF stations scattered through the length and breadth of the country.

As for the aircraft, they were a rather dismal mix of World War I types such as the de Havilland DH9 and Bristol F2B. Operations over the desert meant that crews had to carry numerous external spares wheels, radiators, extra fuel tanks, cameras, water, screw pickets, ropes, tools, rations and so on. The wartime aircraft soldiered on until the late 1920s, after

which they began to be replaced by the Westland Wapiti, a sturdy and popular aircraft that remained in service with the RAF until 1943.

The timing of Air Vice-Marshal Salmond's successful campaign in Iraq was fortuitous. In Whitehall, fierce debates had been raging since 1921 about the whole future of the service, with both Army and Navy commanders insisting that it be subordinated and that separate army and naval air arms should be created from existing RAF forces. This political infighting continued until February 1926, when Prime Minister Stanley Baldwin announced in the House of Commons that the Government had no intention of creating separate air arms and that "it is in the interests of the fighting Services that controversy upon this subject should now cease". Nonetheless, the dispute continued to hamper inter-service relations long after this date. Only in 1937 was it finally decided to grant control of the Fleet Air Arm to the Royal Navy, by which time it was hopelessly obsolete. The independence of the Royal Air Force in the early 1920s resulted from a fortunate conjuncture between the pressures of budget, the need to stabilise Mesopotamia, the political ambitions of Winston Churchill and Trenchard's ambitions for the Service.

While maintaining independence, however, the RAF suffered badly from the financial constraints forced on it. Nowhere was this more true than in Egypt, where the

ABOVE: RAF aircrew pictured as they are ferried back to their Shorts Rangoon flying boat, one of only six built for the RAF, lying off Samahha in the Sea of Galilee in 1933.

squadrons funded by the Indian government were starved of even the most basic resources needed to keep their dilapidated aircraft in the air. Trenchard sent Salmond to India on a tour of inspection in 1922. The report he produced was highly critical, but again there was little more than token acceptance of its recommendations and little was done to actually modernise or extend the useful life of the Indian squadrons' equipment.

THE RAF IN PALESTINE AND ADEN

During the 1920s, flying units played a largely supporting role to ground units in the two other British-controlled territories in the Middle East, Palestine and Aden. Both these areas were far more developed than Iraq or northern India, and here ground forces were obviously better suited for policing work. Air operations were limited to reconnaissance missions or demonstrations of air power to the hostile Arab tribesmen who made regular cross-border incursions into Palestine and Transjordan from French-controlled Syria. Hostility between Arabs and Jews within Palestine eventually came to replace this as the major threat to security in the region, but the effectiveness of aircraft in their inter-communal fighting was limited.

A more successful policing operation was carried out by the RAF in the Aden Protectorate, a small territory of southern Arabia ceded to Britain by the Turks at the Versailles conference. Until 1927, small detachments of the RAF were sufficient to suppress the dissident tribes in the hinterland around the territory, but in 1927 these actions escalated into

a full-scale rebellion as Yemeni irregulars launched an attack to coincide with inter-tribal conflict. No 8 Squadron and a detachment of armoured cars were dispatched from Baghdad in early 1928 and were mounting operations against the dissidents by late February. In a period of intense air activity that lasted until August, No 8 Squadron dropped some 70 tons of bombs and fired off 33,000 rounds of ammunition. Despite some limited action during January and March of 1928, the actions petered out, in some small part due to the operations of the RAF, and for a short time, at least, peace descended on Aden.

THE NORTH-WEST FRONTIER

Mention has already been made of RAF operations on the North-West Frontier during World War I. The Versailles Treaty prompted a temporary ceasefire between the warring factions, but after a brief cessation in hostilities, trouble flared again and continued almost unabated until World War II. Throughout this period life for the RAF personnel stationed on the Frontier was harsh. Living conditions were starkly primitive, and for the average airman they were anything but comfortable.

In July 1924 a joint ground and air offensive was mounted against the dissident Mahsud tribes in south Waziristan. After six months, this proved insufficient to suppress the rebel tribes. In response, it was decided to mount an independent air action against tribal strongholds. These operations began on March 9, 1925 and continued for 54 days, after which the tribal leaders agreed to terms put forward at a peace conference. The RAF contribution to this operation had a positive influence on the allocation of resources and finances to the Service at a time when they were most needed, although opinions of its effectiveness were predictably divided.

The myriad operations in which the six RAF squadrons based in India during the 1930s were engaged are too detailed to list here, and are worthy of a separate study. Notable among them, however, was the evacuation by air of the staff and families of the British Embassy in Kabul, along with nationals of 11 other countries, after a rebellion against the Amir of Afghanistan broke out in December 1928. Also worthy of mention in this brief overview is the attempted overthrow of Peshawar in 1930 by the Mahsud tribes, who

---

WESTLAND WAPITI

Westland began manufacturing the Wapiti in 1927. The aircraft, which was loosely based on the previous DH.9 design, was one of the most hard-used and well-loved aircraft to serve in any air force. Arctic, Long-Range, float and ski versions, target-tugs and dual trainers were built and about 80 remained in India well into World War II.

---

were driven back by repeated air attacks from RAF aircraft. Hostilities along the Frontier continued until the autumn of 1932. The RAF was perhaps the prime military asset in the Middle East at this time and the operations in which it was involved helped to validate its independence at a time of severe budgetary constraint. It must be remembered, though, that many RAF units were still operating aircraft of World War I vintage. Not until February 1932, for example, did No 20 Squadron exchange its F2Bs for Westland Wapitis.

THE ENEMY WITHIN

A disastrous earthquake struck the Frontier territories on May 31, 1935, devastating the RAF station at Quetta. The earthquake coincided with a period of heavy fighting against tribesmen in the Mohmand territory, and hampered RAF operations in the region for some months. In 1936, with RAF strength in India restored, a jihad (holy war) was declared by the Fakir of Ipi on British forces stationed on the Frontier. Air and ground forces were successful in driving the Fakir and his supporters into the hills in November, but during the next 18 months he successfully evaded capture despite an escalation in the size of the forces ranged against him. He died in April 1938, but the anti-British propaganda he stirred up remained a thorn in the side of the Indian government for many years.

The era of air policing was a testing time for the new Service. It was forced to operate in extreme conditions in far-flung corners of British administration with obsolete aircraft and inadequate logistical support. The concept was undoubtedly successful in the early operations in Iraq and Transjordan, preventing possible reoccupation by the Turks. In India, Aden, and on the North-West Frontier too, air policing may be judged a success. In Palestine, internal problems were more complex and the policy had undoubtedly failed by 1936. The effects of aerial bombing on civilian populations could be truly devastating, as was tragically proved in the Spanish Civil War that began in 1936, and there were many critics, with powerful voices in Parliament, who questioned the morality of such actions. In retrospect the idea of bombing tribesmen armed only with rifles seems morally reprehensible, but it is not appropriate to apply modern standards to a different era. It is important to note, however, that these campaigns played no part in forming RAF doctrine, as it was realised from the outset that they had no relevance to a war with a modern power, and were undertaken with obsolete machines. Air policing made a major contribution to the independence of the RAF at a time when its continued existence was in doubt, and gave invaluable experience to many of its aircrews for the coming conflict in Europe.

BUILDING BLOCKS

Between the two World Wars, with most RAF strength on overseas detachment, Trenchard struggled against financial limitations to build a strong framework for the Service. His contribution was not only to keep the service alive in its early days, but manifested itself in the institutions of training and support, the raising of the RAF's image in public estimation, the development of clear doctrines and modern theories of aerial warfare, and in its structure.

The White Paper of 1919 outlined Trenchard's proposal to build a framework for the RAF supported by five institutions of training and support. The first of these was an RAF cadet college that was the equivalent of the Naval and Army colleges at Dartmouth, Sandhurst and Woolwich. The site chosen was the former RNAS training station at Cranwell in Lincolnshire, and it opened in February 1920 with 52 cadets, all of whom were accommodated in the most basic of huts.

Trenchard also threw his support behind the Central Flying School. The School had been in existence for seven years and, although it was originally established as simply a flying training school, had developed into an academy that was at the forefront of aeronautical science. The training techniques of the CFS were based on the principles of dual flying and exploring the flight envelope of an aircraft, a simple logic that proved to be of great benefit to successive generations of graduates.

The paucity of properly trained and qualified air mechanics in the air services was realised during World War I, prompting Trenchard to establish a training camp for the technical trades at Halton. This was the foundation for Trenchard's postwar apprentice scheme, which provided the RAF with a strong skill base. Until permanent facilities were opened at Halton in January 1922 to replace the wartime huts and tents, training was undertaken at Cranwell. The RAF Staff College at Andover was also established to develop the theories and practice of future RAF operations.

THE AUXILIARY AIR FORCE

Trenchard realised that heavy post-war financial pressure on the service would preclude a large permanent force. At the same time, he wished to prevent an erosion in the expertise that had been built up during the War, as this would hamper future expansion. In 1924, the Auxiliary Air Force and Air

BELOW: A Westland Wapiti of No 60 Squadron, Royal Air Force, dropping bombs on a suspected rebel target on the North-West Frontier of India.

ABOVE: The Supermarine S6B in which Flight Lieutenant J N Boothman won the Schneider Trophy outright for Britain on September 12, 1931.

Force Reserve Act was passed, allowing for six Auxiliary squadrons and seven Special Reserve squadrons, the eventual aim being 20 Auxiliary squadrons in total. In an era when flying was growing in popularity, these were well-subscribed and enthusiastically staffed, leading to the popular image of the Royal Auxiliary Air Force as the "best flying club in the world" in the 1930s. Aside from their social status, the Auxiliary squadrons played an extremely important role in World War II.

PUBLIC RELATIONS

The numerous ways devised for publicising the new service were an important means of attracting recruits, and friends, in the inter-war years. The performances of the Central Band of the Royal Air Force (established in April 1920) was one factor, but it is the air displays at Hendon that most readily spring to mind. The displays took place every June from 1920 until 1937, and were incredibly popular, with paying crowds of 60,000 joined by thousands of others watching outside. Formation flying, mock attacks on specially constructed native forts and parachute descents became regular items on the programme. Another very public display of RAF dedication to public service was the establishment of mail

routes and air links between London and Europe, and most famously, Cairo and Baghdad. This latter service was pioneered by RAF pilots across the Arabian desert and was later taken over by Imperial Airways.

Record-breaking and pioneering flights were yet another way of bringing the RAF to public notice, and from 1919 a number of successful attempts at distance, height and speed were undertaken by the RAF. In 1927, for example, four Supermarine Southampton flying boats flew to Australia via India, Singapore and Hong Kong before returning to Singapore to form No 205 Squadron. The image of the RAF in the 1930s is intrinsically linked with the Supermarine aircraft that vied for the Schneider Trophy. This contest – Britain won the Trophy outright in 1931 – captured the public imagination and fostered advances in aeronautical engineering that later proved a considerable advantage to Britain in wartime.

PLANNING FOR WAR

Aside from its public relations mission, the RAF sought to establish the guidelines under which it would fight a future war. During the 1930s, the most prominent theories of the role of an independent air force were based either on the principles of air superiority – that is, denying the enemy the use of the air as a prelude to an attack on his vital centres – or else the strategic theory of simply destroying his centres of production and communication. Emphasis on the principle

HAWKER HIND

During the late 1920s and early 1930s, Sidney Camm designed a very capable family of light bombers for Hawker aircraft. The bi-plane configuration was rapidly becoming obsolete when the Hind entered service in 1935, but it formed an important bridge in the RAF bomber fleet until more advanced types, such as the Vickers Wellington, could be brought into service.

of offence in air operations was popularised by Trenchard and maintained by the Royal Air Force right through the 1920s and up until the last 18 months of peace in 1938–9. In practical terms, this policy meant that emphasis was placed on equipping the RAF with a substantial, but ultimately inadequate, strategic bomber fleet.

The belief that Germany – which after the Nazi party came to power in 1933, emerged as the greatest threat to Britain – would concentrate its rearmament on bomber aircraft, caused great consternation among the British public and press and influenced the Chiefs of Staff in their decision to build up the front-line bomber strength of the RAF, albeit with obsolete aircraft without the range to attack Germany from Britain. The neglect of air defence forces was sorely exposed in the opening months of World War II.

COUNTDOWN TO WAR

The realisation that Britain faced a new threat to her national security resulted in eight prewar rearmament schemes, the first of which was approved by the Cabinet in 1934. This planned to match the Luftwaffe in strength, and concentrated on expanding the bomber fleet. The plan was constantly revised over the following four years, until by 1938 emphasis was finally on fighter production. However, by this stage Germany had taken a very substantial lead in developing modern aircraft, and there were some very worrying deficiencies in British defence planning. First, it was believed that Germany had only limited industrial capacity, and that this would not be bolstered in the event of war by the resources of Western Europe, as happened after 1940; and second, the Chiefs of Staff had not considered the possibility that Britain would also be forced to fight in the Far East.

The lack of a cohesive and modern strategy handicapped the RAF in the late 1930s, although a positive move in 1936 was the consolidation of the RAF into Bomber, Fighter, Coastal and Training Commands. Some significant advances were made in aeronautical technology during this period,

marked by the emergence of all-metal low-wing monoplanes such as the Sidney Camm-designed Hawker Hurricane and the Supermarine Spitfire. The latter aircraft owed much to Supermarine and Rolls Royce experience in the Schneider Trophy races, which lasted from 1913 to 1931, and to the tireless forward thinking and personal sacrifice of its designer Reginald Mitchell.

All too late, as Europe descended into conflict, the Air Ministry realised that it had focused for too long on the light bomber as its primary weapon. This rationale explains why aircraft of such dubious operational value as the Fairey Battle figured so strongly in the RAF inventory in 1939. Only after its mauling in France in 1940 did the RAF acknowledge the poor combat capabilities of its front-line aircraft.

One of the most influential players within the RAF top brass at this time was Air Marshal Hugh Dowding. From 1938, he led Fighter Command and pushed for more capable types to be brought into service. Perhaps his most important contribution to the RAF in the late 1930s, and one that was to be of prime importance in the Battle of Britain, was the establishment of early warning radar sites around the British coast. In March 1935, in a far-sighted move that was to have an incalculable effect on the outcome of the Battle, Dowding (then Air Member for Supply and Organisation) ordered the construction of the first 20 air defence coastal radar stations.

RIGHT: The programme of the 1931 Schneider Trophy Contest, the event that fostered advances in aeronautical engineering and proved to be of incalculable benefit to Britian in the war.

CHAPTER 3

THE BATTLE OF BRITAIN

The Battle of Britain is the only major battle in history to be fought in the air. It was won with a measure each of luck, skill and bravery by the Royal Air Force, and to this day is remembered as its finest hour.

In the summer and autumn of 1940, the RAF was confronted with the sternest test it had yet faced. After the Nazi assault on Western Europe and the humiliating withdrawal of the British Army from Dunkirk in northern France at the end of June, 1940, the RAF, together with ships of the Royal Navy,

ABOVE: Hurricane pilots race to their aircraft to intercept an incoming wave of German aircraft during the Battle of Britain in the summer of 1940.

LEFT: A Squadron intelligence officer (with his back to camera) listens to the account of a Sergeant Pilot standing to his right of a combat only recently ended.

mounted a magnificent and ultimately successful defence against the Nazis' next step: the invasion of Britain. Skilful planning, efficient management of limited resources, excellent command and control, technology, luck and bravery all played vital roles in the struggle, which has been rightly acknowledged as one of the most successful and decisive air battles in history.

At the outbreak of the war on September 3, 1939, the RAF could call on a strength of 114 squadrons. Fighter Command held 39, 25 of them equipped with Hurricanes and Spitfires and the remainder equipped with Gloster Gladiators, Gloster Gauntlets and even a few Hawker Hinds. Bomber Command was the largest force, in line with prewar doctrine, with 920

SUPERMARINE SPITFIRE

The Spitfire is the enduring image of the Battle for most people, and was certainly the most capable fighter aircraft that Fighter Command possessed in 1940. Although in numerical terms the Hurricane was more significant, the Spitfire could match and in some areas outperform the Messerschmitt Bf 109E. and has rightly been recognised as one of the decisive weapons of the War.

aircraft in 55 squadrons. Although on paper this looked an impressive force, ten squadrons of Fairey Battles and two squadrons of Bristol Blenheims were committed to France with the Advanced Air Striking Force and another 17 were withdrawn to form Operational Training Units, leaving a strength of only 352 aircraft. Coastal Command had 10 squadrons, equipped with aircraft ranging from the Shorts Sunderland to the Supermarine Walrus. Opposing them were 4,204 Luftwaffe aircraft, 90 percent of which were serviceable at any time. Despite the hasty rearmament of the late 1930s, many people questioned whether the RAF had the material strength to challenge this force.

In terms of personnel, the RAF had 11,573 officers and 169,939 other ranks. The quality of training was extremely variable, mainly because of inadequate and outmoded equipment. Navigational standards among the bomber crews were very poor. Virtually no all-weather training was undertaken,

and navigational aids were very primitive. In air-to-air gunnery the situation was hardly better. Many gunners had not been properly trained to operate the power turrets fitted to RAF aircraft, which were confidently predicted to render the bombers invulnerable to attack. In marked contrast, many of the German airmen had combat experience obtained during the Spanish Civil War (1936–9) and their tactics were based on experience rather than classroom theory.

THE PHONY WAR

During September 1939, Poland was viciously crushed under the weight of Hitler's blitzkreig (lightning war) and the British population nervously awaited the arrival of German bombers over their own cities. The predicted attacks did not come – yet – and Britain was afforded a temporary respite. This was popularly referred to as the "Phony War", which the British used to fortify air defences including anti-aircraft batteries, shelters, balloons and searchlights, as well as to strengthen their forces.

Bomber Command operations during this period, which lasted seven months until April 1940, were restricted to daylight attacks on the havens of the German fleet and night-time leaflet dropping over Germany, the so-called "Nickel Raids". Few tangible successes were scored, apart from the fact that the RAF proved it could penetrate German airspace. On these missions, the Fairey Battles, Vickers Wellingtons, Armstrong Whitworth Whitleys and Handley Page Hampdens of Bomber Command had no fighter escort and endured heavy losses against German fighter pilots

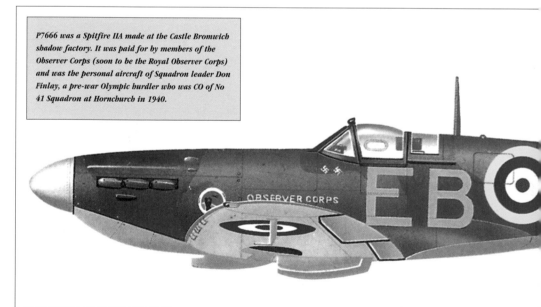

P7666 was a Spitfire IIA made at the Castle Bromwich shadow factory. It was paid for by members of the Observer Corps (soon to be the Royal Observer Corps) and was the personal aircraft of Squadron leader Don Finlay, a pre-war Olympic hurdler who was CO of No 41 Squadron at Hornchurch in 1940.

flying aircraft with cannon armament and with a speed advantage of up to 161 kp/h (100 mph). The heavy losses sustained during daylight raids peaked in December 1939 and made it apparent that losses would rapidly become unsustainable. By comparison, the night-time raids were less expensive in terms of men and aircraft, showing a possible way forward for the bombing offensive.

The pilots of Fighter Command squadrons at home and on deployment in France with the AASF saw little action during this unnerving prelude to the fighting. Few targets of worth appeared over the British positions save the odd German reconnaissance machine. The only really notable development was the creation of a dedicated photo reconnaissance unit within the RAF. As with so many other essential aspects of air operations, photo-reconnaissance had been badly neglected during the 1930s. The RAF were quick to appreciate the value of this intelligence and as the war progressed, its reconnaissance and interpretation units played an increasingly important role in strategic and tactical planning.

NORWAY AND DENMARK

During the invasion of Norway and Denmark, which began on 9 April 1940 and so ended the Phony War, Bomber Command mounted daylight raids against the German invasion fleet, but not a single vessel was hit, let alone sunk. Within hours of the initial airborne and naval assault, German paratroopers secured the important airfields. The loss of the airfields meant that support for the British and French expeditionary forces that came ashore at Namsos,

A pilot officer of Fighter Command at the height of the Battle of France in May 1940. During the Battle of Britain flying clothing was largely a matter of personal choice, but although uncomfortable and bulky, parachute equipment was a statutory requirement for all squadrons.

Aandalsnes and Narvik in the following weeks was severely limited. Attacks against occupied airfields confirmed that daylight operations were highly vulnerable; no fewer than nine of the 83 aircraft sent to attack two German cruisers on April 12 failed to return, and apart from occasional raids by Blenheims of No 2 Group, Bomber Command switched to night-time attacks after this date. The defenders of Norway were overcome by June 4 and an evacuation of men and equipment began.

The RAF was dealt a further devastating blow on June 8, when the eight Hurricanes and eight Gladiators committed to the defence, and successfully evacuated back to the aircraft carrier HMS *Glorious*, were lost, together with almost the entire complement, when the vessel was sent to the bottom of the North Sea by the German battle cruisers *Scharnhorst* and *Gneisenau*.

FRANCE

In May 1940, when the Nazi invasion of Western Europe began, two elements constituted the RAF force on the continent. The Air Component of the British Expeditionary Force was made up of five squadrons of Westland Lysanders for tactical reconnaissance, four squadrons of Blenheims intended for strategic reconnaissance and four squadrons of Hurricanes for air defence. It was by any standards a meagre force and was later strengthened to ten squadrons at the insistence of the French, and much to the reluctance of Hugh Dowding, now Air Officer Commander in Chief, Fighter Command.

The Advanced Air Striking Force had ten squadrons of Fairey Battles and Bristol Blenheims, which were to attack German columns, and four squadrons of Hurricanes for air defence. These squadrons could be allocated to any part of the front, and, to some extent, they could draw on the strength of home-based units.

Opposing them was the most efficient military force of its day. As well as the numerical advantage it enjoyed, the Luftwaffe, the well-equipped and experienced air arm of the German invasion force, could also rely on the vital element of surprise. When the massive air and ground assault on Belgium, the Netherlands, Luxembourg and France began on

May 10, nine of the RAF forward bases were attacked. With 1,150 fighter aircraft at their disposal the Luftwaffe achieved air superiority with ease. Numerous assaults against the advancing German forces were launched by the Battles and Blenheim squadrons over the course of the next 48 hours, but their losses were horrendous. For instance, on May 12, seven of the nine Blenheims of No 139 Squadron which set out to attack an enemy column near Maastricht in the Netherlands failed to return. On that same day, No 12 Squadron was tasked with attacking bridges over the Albert canal near Maastricht. Every member of the squadron volunteered and six aircraft were dispatched. One returned after it had become unserviceable, while the remainder of the force pressed on with their desperate and heroic attack on bridges. One of the two bridges was destroyed but all five aircraft were brought down. For this action two airmen, Flight Officer D E Garland and Sergeant T Gray, were posthumously awarded the Victoria Cross.

RETREAT

In just two days the bomber strength of the AASF was nearly halved. Losses continued to mount in the days that followed. On May 13, the Allied defences were breached and replacement Hurricane pilots were sent to France. On the May 14 the bombing effort was concentrated on pontoon bridges

BELOW: RAF pilots examine a spinner, armament and fuselage panel from a Dornier 17 they have shot down in the Battle of France.

ABOVE: A Lockheed Hudson of Coastal Command approaching Dunkirk during Operation Dynamo. Although it was criticised in the aftermath, the RAF played a full part in the evacuation.

near Sedan; Blenheim losses amounted to 75 percent of those engaged, totalling some 28 aircraft. The next day 40 of the 71 aircraft that took off to attack German positions failed to return. Contrary to Dowding's urgent wishes, Churchill sent reinforcements, but these could not halt the rout and on May 19 the surviving RAF aircraft were flown to England. Yet another disaster befell the RAF during the retreat. One hundred and twenty of the vitally important Hurricane fighters had to be destroyed to prevent their capture. This meant that out of a total of 261 Hurricanes deployed to France only 66 were returned.

OPERATION DYNAMO

Contrary to opinion at the time, the RAF were heavily engaged over the evacuation beaches at Dunkirk during the rescue effort, Operation Dynamo. Dowding foresaw the need to conserve his fighter aircraft for the vital battle over Britain that would clearly follow, but nevertheless, some 2,739 missions were flown, and air superiority over Dunkirk was achieved for much of the time. By the end of the withdrawal on June 4, RAF losses amounted to 959 aircraft – 229 of them AASF, 279 of the BEF Air Component, 219 of Fighter Command, 166 of Bomber Command and 66 of Coastal Command. Far more serious was the fact that between May 10 and June 4, no less than 432 Hurricanes and Spitfires were lost. These losses deeply undermined RAF strength and its capacity to defend Britain from air attack, and did little to bolster the confidence of its pilots.

It is difficult to underestimate the gravity of this situation. The German Führer Adolf Hitler himself believed that Britain was already defeated. His generals were rather more

KEITH PARK

Air Vice-Marshal Keith Park took over command of 11 Group in April 1940 and led it throughout the Battle. He was born in New Zealand and flew over the Western Front during World War I, before becoming Dowding's Senior Air Staff Officer in 1938. His disagreements with Air Marshal Sir Trafford Lee-Mallory over tactics led to great bitterness and he was removed from command once the Battle was won.

the area between East Anglia and West Dorset, including London and the Home Counties. It was this group, commanded by Air Vice-Marshal Keith Park, a tough and resourceful New Zealander, that bore the brunt of the fighting. Each group was divided into sectors: No 11 Group, for example, was made up of seven different sectors, each of which controlled a number of separate airfields.

The radar sites and observer sites were linked via two separate overland links to Air Marshal Dowding's Fighter Command headquarters at Bentley Priory in Middlesex, and to all the group and sector airfields. Acting on the basis of information received, HQ Fighter Command could give an order to intercept to the relevant Group fighter controller. These men were perhaps the key part of the whole system. It was their responsibility to allocate a raid to a particular sector according to the height and direction of the attacking force, and the readiness of the defending aircraft (the operational readiness of each squadron or flight was indicated on a large board in the Operations Room at Bentley Priory). The Controller could then order a particular squadron or squadron flight to scramble and vector it to the interception point via radio.

*ABOVE: **Women's Auxiliary Air Force personnel work the plotting table at 11 Group HQ, RAF Uxbridge. This was the nerve centre of the Battle of Britain, where the major decisions were made.***

cautious but had good reason to feel optimistic of success, provided German troops could be transported safely across the English Channel. They commanded 120 well-equipped divisions, whereas in Britain the army had barely 21, all of them seriously short of arms and equipment. The Royal Navy, which was numerically stronger than the German Kriegsmarine, presented a threat to the invasion fleet, but if air superiority could be achieved over the Channel this could be neatly extinguished. The Luftwaffe was therefore ordered to proceed with all haste in defeating the RAF, in time for a planned invasion date in early autumn.

COMMAND AND CONTROL

At the forefront of Britain's air defence network were the 42 "Chain Home" early warning radar sites – tall, exposed steel towers concentrated along the eastern approaches. The Chain Home network was vital to the successful defence of Britain in 1940 and relied on the efficient command and control systems established prior to the war. Another indispensable link in the air defence chain was the Observer Corps, which manned hundreds of posts around the country.

For the duration of the War, Britain was divided into 4 sections, each the responsibility of a designated Group. No 13 Group covered the north of the country; No 10 Group looked after the south-west; No 12 Group was responsible for the Midlands and the Wash areas; and No 11 Group had

SHORING UP THE DEFENCES

Dowding also had operational control of Anti-Aircraft Command. By the start of the Battle of Britain, this important resource amounted to some 1,000 heavy AA guns and 600 lighter weapons, although this was only approximately half the total required. Augmenting the AA batteries were 1,400 barrage balloons, deployed around vital targets such as

---

HUGH DOWDING

Air Marshal Sir Hugh Dowding led Fighter Command through the Battle of Britain with consummate skill and intelligence. Although he was seemingly distant and aloof from the men he led, they held him in the utmost regard. At the outbreak of the Battle, he was easily the most senior RAF commander but did not enjoy the total support of the Air Ministry. Nevertheless, Dowding was made a Knight, Grand Cross of the Order of the Bath (GCB) in 1940 and was granted a barony in 1943.

LEFT: Air Chief Marshal Sir Hugh Dowding, to whom much of the credit for the eventual victory in the Battle must go, was hastily removed from office in November 1940.

BELOW: Hawker Hurricanes flying in the vic-formation that was taught to all trainee fighter pilots. This formation was decidedly inferior to the Luftwaffe Rotte and Schwarm tactic.

airframe and engine works to deter low-level and dive-bombing attacks. As mentioned previously, the strength of the RAF had been seriously depleted both in terms of men and machines during the Battle of France. The shortfall in aircraft was made good in the two months after Dunkirk, largely through the energies of the dynamic newspaper proprietor Max Beaverbrook, who was appointed by Prime Minister Churchill to head a new Ministry of Aircraft Production. By the middle of August, 700 aircraft were available, and production levels were increasing.

Pilots, however, were not so easily replaced. Despite the fact that the RAF had been strengthened by squadrons of volunteer Czech and Polish pilots, and by men from Canada, New Zealand, Australia, South Africa, India, the West Indies, and America, by mid-August Dowding still lacked 154 pilots.

While Britain made good its defences, the Luftwaffe sought to recover its own strength. Aircraft losses of nearly 40 percent had been sustained in eight months of successive campaigning. Recovery was ominously swift. The most reliable sources estimated the total combat strength of the

REICHSMARSHALL HERMANN GÖRING

Reichsmarshall Hermann Göring led the Luftwaffe throughout World War II, and was responsible for many key tactical decisions during the course of the Battle. He was a close friend and associate of Adolf Hitler, though the Luftwaffe's failure in 1940 cooled their relationship, which never recovered. During the latter part of World War I, Göring had commanded the élite Richthofen squadron, but his tactical naïveté proved to be a key factor in the outcome of the Battle.

Luftwaffe by mid-August at 1,481 twin-engine bombers, 327 dive bombers, 289 twin-engine fighters and 934 single-engine fighters.

TACTICS

Numerical superiority was not the only advantage the German pilots enjoyed. The tactics employed by the RAF at this time were better suited to air displays than the rigours of

BELOW: A German bomb that fell without exploding on the parade ground at RAF Helmswell on August 27, 1940, is safely detonated by the station armaments officer.

aerial combat. Pre-training focused on disciplined flying in Vee formations, a legacy of the prewar belief that air combat would be a question of fighter against bomber. Instead of maintaining a vigilant lookout for enemy aircraft a pilot had to expend his energies trying to keep station. Although many squadrons adopted their own tactics from the lessons of experience, important differences of opinion divided the Group commanders of Nos 11 and 12 Group, Keith Park and Trafford Leigh-Mallory, which would have better been resolved before the War.

The Luftwaffe, drawing on their experiences in the Spanish Civil War, used a different system based on a mutually supporting pair of aircraft called a Rotte. In this formation, the wingman flew to the side and behind his leader and was responsible for guarding the rear, leaving the lead man to direct all attention on the sky ahead. Pairs of Rotte were known as a Schwarm. These formations were far more flexible and manouevrable than the Fighter Command "'vic", and enabled all four pilots to keep a good lookout while staying in formation.

ADLERTAG (EAGLE DAY)

During July and early August 1940, the Luftwaffe harassed Britain's Channel ports and the convoy shipping bringing coal from northern pits. These attacks were a prelude to the main strike that was planned for August 10, code-named

ABOVE: A high street RAF recruiting office in 1940. There was no shortage of volunteers for the RAF during the Battle, but a very real lack of experienced pilots.

Adlertag (Eagle Day). The aim of this operation, laid down by Hitler in Directive No 17 of August 1, was to "destroy the Royal Air Force using all available force against primarily the flying units, their ground facilities and their support, but also the aviation industry, including that manufacturing anti-aircraft equipment. "

Poor weather on August 10 forced a postponement, and only on August 12 did the German attacks begin. Heavily escorted formations of bombers attacked radar stations and airfields near the English south coast. Five radar facilities were damaged, but all but one of them, Ventnor on the Isle of Wight, was back in operation within a few hours. Of the airfields, Manston was put out of action and operations at Hawkinge and Lympne were seriously disrupted.

The following day saw the start of the onslaught proper. Two major attacks were launched against airfields in the south and south-east, causing minor damage for the loss of 45 aircraft, most of them the vulnerable, if terrifying, Ju 87s. By comparison the RAF lost 13 aircraft, and three pilots. August 15 saw another day of heavy fighting, with attacks by all three Luftflotten (air fleets) on targets in the north, east and south. In the late morning a force of 110 Ju 87s and 50 Bf 109s attacked airfields in the south-east, badly damaging Lympne. Another three-pronged attack by 170 aircraft was plotted by radar in the afternoon, but the strength of the defenders deflected many of these raiders from their intended targets. Later in the afternoon, a force of approximately 250 aircraft was intercepted along the southern coast,

JOHN NICHOLSON, VC

The only Victoria Cross to be awarded to a Fighter Command pilot during the Battle was won by Flight Lieutenant John Nicholson of No 249 Squadron, stationed at Boscombe Down in Wiltshire. While on patrol in Hurricane P3576 on August 16, 1940, Nicholson engaged a patrol of enemy Bf 110s and Junkers 88s off the coast near Gosport. His aircraft was attacked and set on fire by escorting Messerschmitt 109s but he pressed on and suffered serious burns as a result. Nicholson survived the Battle and was awarded the Victoria Cross, but was killed in May 1945.

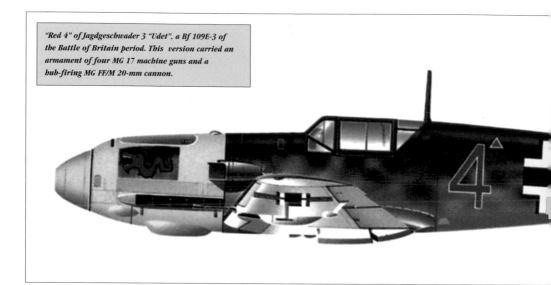

"Red 4" of Jagdgeschwader 3 "Udet", a Bf 109E-3 of the Battle of Britain period. This version carried an armament of four MG 17 machine guns and a hub-firing MG FF/M 20-mm cannon.

and the raid had only very limited effect. In the early evening a raid by 90 Dornier D0 17s escorted by 130 Bf 109s and a diversionary force of 60 Me-109s crossed the Channel. Ten RAF squadrons intercepted, but some of the attacking aircraft were able to penetrate well inland and cause damage at West Malling and Croydon. In total, the number of sorties flown that day by the Luftwaffe amounted to 1,750. Reichsmarshall Hermann Göring, the former World War I air ace, and now commander of the Luftwaffe, made a crucial decision that day, to discontinue attacks on the radar sites, as these had so far produced few tangible results. In retrospect, this proved to be one of the most basic of his many mistakes.

On August 16 a temporary let-up in the fighting gave the RAF time to count their losses and make good the damage as best they could. Between August 8 and August 17, Fighter Command had lost some 154 aircraft, yet fighter production at this time was running at approximately 100 a week. More importantly, 154 pilots were lost in the same period. Only 63

MESSERSCHMITT BF 109

The standard fighter of the Luftwaffe throughout World War II was the Messerschmitt Bf 109. This aircraft came into service in 1937 and was thoroughly combat-proven during the Spanish Civil War. Although marginally less manoeuvrable than the Spitfire, the Me-109 had better performance at altitude and benefited from a fuel injection system. The majority of Luftwaffe Jagdgeschwader were equipped with the 109E model during the Battle.

---

pilots were available as replacements, and they were mostly inexperienced. The other commands were trawled for replacements, but even with these men and the foreign and Commonwealth volunteers, aircrew losses remained the most serious problem Dowding faced.

THE BATTLE OF ATTRITION

This pattern of attack continued almost unabated until September 6. With the exception of a brief spell between August 19–23, when bad weather restricted daytime Luftwaffe operations, there was not a single day when less than 600 sorties were flown against targets in Britain. During the lull, large formations of bombers made night-time attacks on targets from South Wales and Liverpool to East Anglia. One of these formations mistakenly bombed London, prompting the Cabinet to order a retaliatory attack on Berlin on August 25/26. Although this caused little material damage, the attack was to have great significance. Daylight raids recommenced on August 24, with renewed attacks on the RAF bases at Manston, Hornchurch and North Weald, as well as Dover, Ramsgate, Portsmouth and other centres. All the airfields round London were subjected to repeated attack in the next two weeks, sometimes as many as three a day.

Although it is sometimes assumed that the RAF had been brought to its knees by September 6, and that two further weeks of attacks would have been sufficient to seal its fate, the reality is rather more complex. In fact the RAF could draw on large reserves of aircraft from No 13 Group and the rate of aircraft production in Britain was now double what the Germans could manage. Even more crucial, the Luftwaffe were losing far more aircrew every day, either captured or

killed, than the RAF. RAF pilots were regularly rotated to relieve them of combat stress. Those pilots who were available to the Luftwaffe were almost constantly in the front line, and suffered as a result. Although intelligence reports were continually assuring them that the RAF was down to its last 150 aircraft, it was clear that the RAF still possessed a formidable force.

BATTLE OVER LONDON

On September 7 Hitler ordered the Luftwaffe to concentrate its attacks on London. In the mistaken belief that the RAF could no longer offer effective opposition, he lunged hastily to deliver the coup de grace. Göring supported the change in tactics, but it was roundly derided by the weary fighter pilots. They recognised that forcing the fighter units to perform escort duties for the bomber formations would leave both vulnerable to attack. The Messerschmitt Bf 109E had a limited combat range and the fighters would be forced to abandon their escort duties in order to ensure a safe return to France. The twin-engined Bf 110 fighter had a longer range, but was outclassed by both the Hurricane and Spitfire. This in turn would leave the lumbering bomber fleets to the mercy of the RAF on the return flight to France.

The first German attacks concentrated on the docks, the industrial areas and the East End of London. Ineffective airborne radar and a paucity of night-fighting aircraft in the

BELOW: Pilots of an unidentified unit at Biggin Hill in November 1940 display a souvenir from one of their victims. The RAF scored relatively few victories during the night-time Blitz.

RAF meant that very few enemy raiders were intercepted and brought down during the night-time assaults. The raids on London continued through the second week of September, although with nothing like the intensity of the first night. Bombs fell on many different parts of London, including the Admiralty, the War Office and Buckingham Palace.

On September 15, the Battle of Britain reached its zenith. During the late morning a huge German formation gathered over France before setting course for London. Heavy fighting took place over the Home Counties as the bombers flew toward their target. Later in the afternoon, three more waves of attackers came in, a total force of some 200 bombers escorted by 300 fighters. No fewer than 31 RAF squadrons rose to intercept the third wave, but many of the aircraft reached the London area and their bombs caused widespread damage and heavy casualties. Although claims were understandably exaggerated at the time, modern research has shown that the Luftwaffe lost 60 aircraft that day, compared to an RAF loss of 26.

Far more significant than these statistics is the fact that the Luftwaffe was still opposed by nearly 300 RAF aircraft after a month of attacks. While the RAF seemed to be growing stronger, many Luftwaffe pilots were showing signs of combat fatigue in the face of such concerted opposition. On

September 18, Hitler postponed Operation Seelöwe (Operation Sealion), the invasion of Britain, indefinitely and restricted his bomber force to night-time operations. High level daylight raids by fighter-bombers and fighters continued until the October 31, and these posed many problems for the defenders. Not least among these was the inability of the radar network to measure the height of the incoming raids, which could amount to 1,000 sorties in one day, but as October drew to a close these raids became increasingly infrequent and attention switched firmly to night-time bombing – the "Blitz".

THE BLITZ

The much-vaunted Luftwaffe had failed before the first appreciable air force it had encountered, and after losing the war of attrition against the RAF, Hitler turned his attentions to British cities. He believed that attacks against major population centres would destroy the will of the British people to continue fighting and as a result, through the autumn and winter of 1940–1, thousands of tons of bombs were indiscriminately dropped on the British mainland. Worst hit was London, but countless other towns from Liverpool to Portsmouth experienced the terror of these attacks. The RAF could do little to prevent them prior to the arrival of effective airborne radar. Between September 7 and November 13 night fighters managed to shoot down only eight enemy aircraft. The total for all the defences combined amounted to less than one percent of sorties dispatched.

A raid on Coventry on the night of November 14/15 killed 554 people and seriously injured another 865. These figures seem modest in comparison with later operations, but at the time they were considered extremely grave. Considerable effort was expended in devising effective passive means to counter the German radio navigation systems, Knickbein and X-Gerat, and in constructing dummy targets. More important than these passive measures were the improvements in the night-fighter force. This was equipped with Hurricanes, Spitfires and a few radar-equipped Blenheims, later supplemented by the Boulton-Paul Defiant with its dorsal turret, and the heavily armed Bristol Beaufighter. Despite the arrival of new and better aircraft the campaign against the Luftwaffe during the Blitz could hardly be considered a success. The relentless bombing was brought to a halt not by the actions of the night fighter squadrons, but the redeployment of much of the Luftwaffe to the east in

*BELOW: **During a lull in the Battle, Spitfire pilots relax in the Nissen hut that doubles as their squadron restroom. The age limit on squadron commanders was 28.***

ABOVE: Soldiers stand guard over the wreckage of a Dornier 17Z of 9/KG 76 that was brought down on farmland just outside Biggin Hill after attacking Kenley on August 18, 1940.

preparation for Operation Barbarossa, the invasion of Russia on June 22, 1941.

From June 1941 only about a quarter of Luftwaffe operational strength was deployed in occupied Western Europe and Germany, and the pressure on air defence in Britain was greatly reduced. In the event, three key factors worked to the RAF's advantage. First, the early warning system partly robbed the Luftwaffe of the vital element of surprise. Second, the fact that the Battle was fought over southern Britain meant that Luftwaffe pilots who baled out were out of the war, whereas RAF airmen could reasonably expect to rejoin

the battle, barring serious injury. Coupled with this the RAF also possessed an excellent repair network, which ensured that many seriously damaged aircraft could be returned to service with all possible haste. Some 35 percent of the aircraft delivered to Fighter Command during the Battle were salvaged machines. In addition, German fighters could, on average, spend only about 25 minutes over their targets if they were going to be assured of flying safely back to home base. Third, the combat radius of the Luftwaffe's single most important fighter, the Messerschmitt Bf 109E, was only 200km (125 miles). This meant that although the Jagdgeschwader (single-seat fighter units) could escort the bomber formations as far as London, they had precious little fuel for combat. There was, too, the awful suspense of not knowing whether or not their last drops of fuel would get them home.

"There were only a few of us," First-Lieutenant von Hahn of I/JG 3 reported, "who had not yet had to ditch in the Channel with a shot up aircraft or stationary airscrew."

> "We never thought for a moment that this would be the end of England. It hadn't occurred to me, or to us pilots, that we would lose, and that this was the Battle of Britain; that realisation came later. It was just a lot more fighting for us pilots, after the Battle of France and Dunkirk."
>
> *Air Marshal Sir Denis Crowley-Milling*
> *KCB, CBE, DSO, DFC, AE.*

CHAPTER 4

DISTANT SKIES

Although during the 1930s Britain made little provision for the defence of its vital trading links through the Mediterranean and North Africa, from late 1940 the RAF was faced with a concerted Axis challenge in what was one of the most bitterly contested theatres of the war.

When Il Duce, Benito Mussolini, committed his country to war on June 10, 1940, he envisaged sharing the spoils of Britain's defeat and adding her African and Mediterranean possessions to Italy's own colonies in the area, so forming a great Italian empire. British interest in the region focused on the Suez Canal, the vitally important link to the resources of India and the Far East, but despite extensive operations in the

ABOVE: An RAF ground crew man chalks up a legend on the side of a Spitfire procaiming the 1,000th kill for Malta's air defences.

LEFT: RAF ground crew working on a Bristol Beaufort torpedo bomber in a revetment on Malta in 1943. Beauforts were extensively used in operations over the Mediterranean against Axis shipping convoys plying between Italy and Tripoli.

Middle East during the 1930s, in June 1940 RAF strength in the region amounted to only about 300 aircraft. The operational commander of RAF Middle East, Air Chief Marshal Sir Arthur Longmore, realised that this was a pitifully small force with which to defend an area that included Egypt, the Sudan, Kenya, Palestine and Gibraltar. He also knew that with the crisis at home, he could expect precious few reinforcements. Longmore's force comprised 14 bomber squadrons, nine of them equipped with Bristol Blenheims, four maritime squadrons, two of which operated Sunderlands and five fighter squadrons, none of them equipped with anything better than Gloster Gladiator biplanes. Making up the rest of the force were an extraordinary mixture of Fairey Battles, Vickers Wellesleys, Vickers Vincents, Hawker Audaxes, Hawker Harts and other types of even older vintage. To

exacerbate the problem, the aircraft were widely dispersed across the command.

Opposing them, the Italian air force had some 282 aircraft stationed in Libya, from where the first attack against the Egyptian garrison was expected. A further 150 were stationed in Italian East Africa, but the main force of 1,200 was held in southern Italy, within easy flying distance of Egypt and the important British bases in Malta. Longmore knew that lengthy preparations would be necessary before the Italians could mount an attack on Egypt, and that when they did strike he would need replacement aircraft. A limited number of crated aircraft was available for delivery, but to run the gauntlet of the powerful Italian fleet and air force in the central Mediterranean was clearly too hazardous and the route around southern Africa was prohibitively slow. Alternatively, aircraft could be flown out via Gibraltar and Malta, but this method had its own hazards. In the event crated aircraft were sent by sea to the Gold Coast and after assembly were flown across the barren deserts of northern Africa to Egypt. This operation began on August 24, 1940 and continued to supply British forces in North Africa for the duration of the war.

ITALY STRIKES

By September 1940, 165,000 Commonwealth troops were opposed by 500,000 of the enemy in the Western Desert, a vast barren area at the north-west tip of the African continent. There were further substantial Italian forces in Eritrea and Abyssinia, comprising some 200,000 men. General Sir Archibald Wavell, Commander-in-chief of Allied Forces in the Middle East, justifiably feared his position. If the Italians attacked on all fronts there seemed little he could do to pre-

vent their advance to Cairo, the Egyptian capital, and on to the Canal. Wavell's opponent, however, was the timid Marshal Rodolfo Graziani, not a man for bold strokes. He refused to launch an offensive until a highly agitated Mussolini threatened to remove his command. In September the Italian Tenth Army advanced tentatively into Egypt from Cyrenaica in Libya. Sollum on the north coast fell, followed by Sidi Barrani, where the Italians constructed a series of fortified encampments.

GREECE

On October 28, 1940, with his forces in North Africa delaying their attack on Egypt, Mussolini invaded Greece through

THE ISLAND AIRCRAFT CARRIER

The strategic value of the island of Malta was clear to both the Axis powers, Germany and Italy. As a vital staging post for the British Mediterranean Fleet, and a haven for convoys resupplying the Eighth Army, it became the subject of almost continual attack from the summer of 1940. At the time Italy entered the War, the air defence fleet amounted to five antiquated Swordfish biplanes used for reconnaissance work and three Gladiators. During the first major air assault on Malta, which coincided with the Italian invasion of Greece, these three aircraft, nicknamed Faith, Hope and Charity, made a useful contribution to the defence. For the duration of the German campaign in North Africa, the three RAF airfields on the island and Grand Harbour in the capital, Valletta, were heavily bombed from German bases in Sicily, only 129km (80 miles) to the north. Malta was also an important base from which attacks on German and Italian shipping were launched.

LEFT: RAF Wellington bombers come under attack from Axis aircraft in their blast pens at a Maltese airfield, a scene that was repeated countless times between 1941 and 1943.

inflicted some notable defeats on the Italian Army until the following spring. Some offensive activity was launched from Malta, through whose airfields Wellingtons were being routed as reinforcements to Egypt. By April 6, 1941, the Italian Army had still failed to deliver victory to Il Duce and the Germans invaded the Balkans to resolve the issue. This was prompted by Hitler's fear that the RAF would use airfields in Egypt to launch airstrikes against the precious oilfields of his ally, Romania. The German invasion force consisted of 27 divisions supported by 1,200 aircraft. Despite the arrival of four more RAF squadrons from Egypt, two of Blenheim light bombers, one of Hurricanes and another a mixture of Hurricanes and Lysander reconnaissance aircraft together with reinforcements from Malta, the odds were overwhelming. After nine days of fighting, only 46 RAF aircraft remained serviceable and on April 20 the remainder of the British force was evacuated. RAF flying boats proved invaluable during this operation, but it was clear to everyone that the whole Greek campaign had been a costly folly.

neighbouring Albania. Although Longmore was reluctant to weaken his slender resources, he found himself required to dispatch a force to aid the Greeks. This comprised No 30 Squadron, equipped with a mixture of Blenheims, bombers and fighters. Ground attack operations carried out by these aircraft proved a useful asset to the Greek Army, who

BELOW: Hurricane IIcs of the Desert Air Force in flight over the Western Desert. The IIc was equipped with four 20mm Hispano cannon and, in desert theatres, an 'Aboukir' engine intake filter.

LEFT: Hurricane pilots of No 73 Squadron, RAF in North Africa in 1941. Normal RAF dress codes were relaxed in deference to the gruelling weather conditions.

38,000 already in British hands. It was the first significant British victory of the war and did much to improve the men's morale.

GERMANY ENTERS THE BATTLE

The celebrations were short-lived. Hitler was fully aware of the strategic significance of the North African oil reserves and the Suez Canal. On February 14, 1941, the first of the units that came to be known as the Afrika Korps began arriving in Tripoli. To command this desert army Hitler appointed General Erwin Rommel, later known to the Allies as the "Desert Fox". Rommel was one of his foremost tacticians. Rommel had at his disposal some 150 aircraft; about 50 of them were Bf 109Es transferred with their experienced aircrew from the Channel coast of France. Their arrival quickly enabled the Luftwaffe to destroy the air superiority the RAF had gained. In spite of the slenderness of his resources, Rommel went on the offensive on March 21, attacking the long and vulnerable British line which stretched from the

SLENDER VICTORY

In the Western Desert, British forces counter-attacked on December 9, 1940, driving the Italian Army back across northern Cyrenaica in a series of spectacular victories masterminded by Major-General Richard O'Connor, commander of the Western Desert Force. The RAF presence in Egypt had been reinforced by two squadrons of Wellingtons and one of Hurricanes, while another Hurricane and three Blenheim squadrons had been transferred from the Suez Canal area. The Italian ports of Tobruk, Benghazi, Bardia and Derna were all bombed from Egypt, while Wellingtons from Malta attacked Tripoli and intercepted merchant ships crossing the Mediterranean to supply the Italian forces. Few Italian aircraft were encountered over the battle area, enabling RAF aircraft to roam with impunity and making it possible for the Hurricanes to switch from air defence to the ground attack role. On January 22, 1941, the Italian fort at Tobruk fell. A total of 27,000 Italian troops were captured, to add to the

BELOW: Hurricane Mk IVs taxying in the desert. The Mk IV was the last Hurricane variant in British service and, as seen on the aircraft pictured, it could be fitted with underwing 40mm cannon.

HAWKER HURRICANE IID

By 1942 the Hurricane was becoming outclassed by the newer aircraft appearing over Western Europe, but two developments gave the aircraft a new lease of life in the Western Desert and in Burma. One was the introduction of air-to-ground ballistic rockets and the other was the adoption of the 40mm cannon as an aircraft weapon for ground attack. Hurricane IIDs carrying these weapons were the first RAF aircraft capable of delivering heavy and accurate firepower in direct support of ground forces.

Nile to Beda Fomm. The Greek campaign had considerably weakened RAF strength, which in any event could not withstand Rommel's blitzkreig. Strenuous efforts were made against enemy airfields and troop concentrations, while on the ground the situation grew steadily worse. El Agheila, Agedabia and Benghazi in Libya fell in rapid succession. Within two weeks, the British were driven back as far as Egypt, leaving only Tobruk to hold out against the Afrika Korps.

The Allies were determined to prevent the vital port of Tobruk from falling into German hands. The first German attacks were launched on April 10. Defending Tobruk were 15,000 Australian infantry under Major-General Leslie Morshead, who could take advantage of the extensive works prepared by the Italians. Two squadrons of Hurricanes, Nos 6 and 73, had been left to operate within the perimeter of the defences, while Nos 3, 45 and 55 Squadrons were pulled back to Egypt. The defenders repulsed repeated assaults until Rommel decided to set up a cordon around the town, and laid siege for two months while his forces regrouped. For the Allies, the position now looked grim. Tobruk was a vital link in their supply lines and to lose it would certainly spell disaster in North Africa. Nor was the vital importance of holding Egypt lost on the Commonwealth forces, who after consolidating their defensive positions in Egypt, began a desperate race to reinforce.

REORGANISATION

The logistical difficulties faced by both sides during the Desert War were enormous. Supply lines stretched across the desert and grew longer with each advance. Virtually all resupply was by sea and control of the central Mediterranean was bitterly disputed by the opposing forces. In the baking heat and dust, the Luftwaffe began to suffer serious reliability

CURTISS KITTYHAWK

The Kittyhawk was one of numerous American types operated by the Royal Air Force during World War II. Its performance in air-to-air combat was indifferent, but as a ground attack aircraft, the Kittyhawk excelled. The rugged construction of the airframe and robust engine made it an ideal machine for desert operations.

problems compounded by the fact that by the summer of 1941 German supply lines were stretched to breaking point across North Africa. In the Mediterranean, the Germans' supply convoys were sought out by RAF PR units based at Malta and attacked by anti-shipping aircraft. In November 1941, 14 of the 21 ships sent from Italy were sunk.

The problems were not confined to the Axis forces, however, for on top of its almost continual supply problems, the RAF in the Middle East at this time was in dire need of effective organisation. One of the most pressing problems was that of technical support. Conditions in the desert were particularly hard on machinery, and the only source of spares was the long and vulnerable supply route from Britain. In May 1941 Air Vice-Marshal Graham Dawson was sent to the theatre to organise a more effective engineering infrastructure. He quickly established workshops capable of manufacturing spare parts and carrying out complex engineering work; this enabled the RAF to increase its front line strength from 200 to almost 600 aircraft in November 1941.

BELOW: An American-built Curtiss Kittyhawk of the Desert Air Force taxying through a sandstorm, created by its own propwash, with the aid of a mechanic.

ABOVE: North African ground personnel and an RAF NCO fuel up a Lockheed Hudson Mk V in preparation for another reconaissance mission over the Mediterranean.

Another key change was the successful organisation of air/ground operations with the establishment of Air Support Control Units. These were mobile, jointly manned units located at the headquarters of each Army Corps, with links to the HQ Western Desert Air Force and the HQs of the RAF Wings.

On November 18, 1941 the reinforced British and Commonwealth troops opened another offensive. The 49 squadrons under the command of Air Marshal Sir Arthur Tedder rapidly gained air superiority and the Axis forces were driven back as far as El Agheila, successfully raising the siege of Tobruk and recapturing Benghazi. By retreating, Rommel's supply lines were halved, however, and in December two convoys carrying vital stocks of aviation fuel and other supplies reached Tripoli. Hampered by the diversion of much of the RAF strength to the Far East, the British advance petered out. In January 1942, 400 German aircraft of

Fliegerkorps X arrived in Sicily and began systematically bombing RAF airfields on Malta, the source of damaging attacks against Axis shipping in the Mediterranean. Consequently, with the RAF under siege in Malta, supplies poured into Tripoli.

On May 26, 1942, Rommel launched a massive counter-offensive. Despite the considerable efforts of Air Vice-Marshal Sir Arthur Coningham's Desert Air Force, which engaged the enemy both on the ground and in the air, the Germans made rapid advances all along the Gazala-Bir Hakeim line. The speed of the retreat forced RAF squadrons to operate from wherever the existence of suitable airstrips made it possible, but the withdrawal rapidly turned into a headlong rout. The only positive note was that attacks on Malta eased off as German aircraft based in Sicily and southern Italy were redeployed in support of this attack and also to the Russian Front. After an intense aerial bombardment and dwindling ammunition supplies had sapped the capabilities of the hardy defenders of Tobruk, the last symbol of British strength in North Africa, the Afrika Korps captured the town on June 21. Nearly 30,000 Allied troops were taken prisoner, together with vital stores.

EL ALAMEIN

The British decided to make their last stand at El Alamein, barely 88 km (55 miles) west of Alexandria and the Suez Canal. Allied troops were entrenched along a position flanked to the south by the impassable Qattara depression. This forced Rommel to make a frontal attack with extremely limited forces, and by June 16 they had been repulsed with heavy losses. The Allied Chief-in-Command General Sir

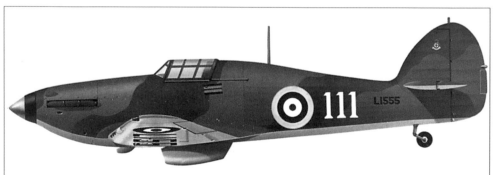

Ninth production Hurricane I (L1555) of No 111 (Fighter) Squadron, Northolt, December 1937. Carrying the CO's pennant, this aircraft was flown by Squadron Leader John ("Downwind") Gillan. Note the absence of ventral fin fairing that was added in 1938 and was characteristic of the Hurricane in later years.

Claude Auchinleck counterattacked on June 21, but made little impression on the Afrika Korps.

In July the air offensive against Malta resumed, but with 200 aircraft available to them, the defenders were able to put up a stout resistance. Some 567 Axis aircraft were ranged against the RAF force; by August 14, 44 of these, together with their crews, had been lost. Against that the RAF had lost 39 aircraft, but 26 of the pilots survived to fight again.

Perhaps realising the desperation of the position in North Africa, Prime Minister Winston Churchill visited the beleaguered British troops in Egypt on August 5, appointing Lieutenant-General Bernard Montgomery as Chief-in-Command in Auchinleck's place. Montgomery and Air Chief Marshal Tedder established a good working relationship that greatly facilitated the effective tactical use of aircraft for the rest of the campaign.

By September 2, the German attacks at El Alamein had been called off. Rommel's supply lines across the Mediterranean were under heavy attack by the Royal Navy and the RAF, starving him of the one commodity that he desperately needed – fuel. Axis attacks on well-dug positions around El Alamein were proving too costly, both in terms of fuel and equipment. The Allied forces, bolstered by American Army Air Force units from India, as well as by a steady flow of reinforcements for the Eighth Army, now prepared to attack.

On October 23, the Second Battle of El Alamein began at 9.40 pm. A huge 882-gun artillery barrage pounded the German lines, prior to the advance of infantry. Ninety-six squadrons were available to the Allies, 60 of them RAF and Fleet Air Arm units. Three weeks prior to the attack, Tedder had launched an attack that decimated Axis forces on the ground. This left only 690 aircraft available to the Luftwaffe in North Africa, although nearly 2,300 were spread across the rest of the Mediterranean. The massive air superiority now enjoyed by the Allies was a key feature of the battle. While medium bombers made constant attacks on enemy positions, fighter-bombers attacked armour without fear of interception by enemy fighters. The fighting was locked in stalemate until November 3, when Rommel, whose forces were critically short of petrol and ammunition, ordered a withdrawal. Two days later, a furious Hitler signalled Rommel to halt the withdrawal, but the logistical position the Desert Fox faced left him with few other options.

The final blow for the Afrika Korps was struck at 5.15 am on November 8, 1942, when over 100,000 men of the Central, Western and Eastern task forces of Operation Torch began to land on the beaches of Morocco, Algeria, and Tunisia. They included the Americans, who were about to experience their first major campaign outside the Pacific theatre since entering the War at the end of 1941. Hitler was forced to send reinforcements to Rommel, now sandwiched between two armies far greater in strength than his own. Despite difficult conditions, and severely handicapped both by poor logistic and maintenance facilities and by lack of suitable airfields, squadrons of RAF Spitfires struggled to support the Allied forces as they fought their way through Tunisia. Winter rains and determined resistance from the Luftwaffe bogged down the western advance in December. In the Mediterranean, heavily armed Bristol Beauforts and Vickers Wellingtons destroyed almost every Italian vessel that ventured onto its waters.

VICTORY IN AFRICA

Throughout the winter of 1942–3, Rommel led his Afrika Korps in a skilful retreat to Tunis, their vital port of supply. The Allied First Army pushed the Germans to within 48km (30 miles) of Tunis by January 1943. In January, Tedder was

Shown with centreline 227-kg (500-lb) bomb, this Kittyhawk Mk III, FR 241, of No 112 (Fighter) Squadron, RAF, flew with No 239 Wing based at Cutella, Italy, during the first five months of 1944; by that time the "sand and spinach" camouflage scheme was standard in the Mediterranean theatre.

ABOVE: ***RAF Martin Baltimore bombers flying over the coast of Malta on their way to attack enemy positions in Sicily in July 1943.***

appointed overall commander of all Allied air units in the region. Prior to his appointment, the chains of command had been somewhat disjointed. Winter rain hampered further movements, so Lieutenant-General Kenneth Anderson, in command of the First Army, dug in to wait for the arrival of the US II Corps. The Eighth Army continued their march up the coast throughout January and February, forcing Rommel into a narrower and narrower pocket. On April 22, the combined forces of Anderson and Montgomery attacked German lines. Rommel had flown to Germany on March 9 to beg Hitler to let him evacuate his men, but his pleas fell on deaf ears. The Führer replaced the Desert Fox with General Jürgen von Arnim, but the new commander was in a hopeless position. Tunis fell on May 7, and by May 14 all the Axis forces in North Africa were in captivity.

THE ITALIAN CAMPAIGN

The decision to invade Italy in July 1943 was not universally popular amongst the Allies. At the Casablanca conference attended by Churchill and US President Franklin D Roosevelt in January 1943, Churchill had expressed his view that the Italians were on the brink of capitulating, that the Allies would effectively have control of the Mediterranean if Italy was occupied, and that by pressing the Axis on another front, they would be forced to divert much-needed resources. The Russian leader, Josef Stalin, was unable to attend the conference due to commitments at Stalingrad, but urged Churchill and Roosevelt to open a second front in

Western Europe to ease the pressure on his much-beleaguered country. Churchill triumphed, and plans for Operation Husky, the invasion of Sicily, were made during the spring.

SICILY

For six weeks prior to the planned invasion day, July 10, 1943, airfields, ports and industrial targets on Sicily, Sardinia and in southern Italy were the subject of continual Allied air attacks by the Strategic Air Force.

On July 10, some 180,000 men of the US Seventh Army and British Eighth Army landed on the shores of Sicily, off the south-western coast of Italy. Complete air cover was assured by the deployment of 4,000 Allied aircraft. The RAF contingent in this huge aerial armada was represented by 121 squadrons. The Axis forces, for their part, could muster only 550. The Allied air forces were given four main task: first, to gain air superiority; second, to give air cover to the convoys at sea; third, to operate over the beach-heads so as to provide cover for Allied ships offshore, and to attack enemy defences on shore; and fourth, to support the subsequent advance of the armies through Sicily.

The Eighth Army, under Montgomery, met with little opposition at their landing point just south of Syracuse on the south-east coast. Resistance at the Gulf of Gila, disembarkation point for the US forces, was stiffer but easily overcome. Syracuse fell on July 12, but Montgomery's direct drive to Messina on Sicily's north-eastern coast faltered in the face of determined German defences around Catania. The US forces, under General George S Patten, were hampered by the hilly Sicilian terrain, and he chose instead to make a looping attack around the northern coast, taking Palermo on July 22. Units of the US 3rd division reached Messina on August 22, shortly after the German evacuation across the straits to Italy, 87km (54miles) away. Although the Germans had lost 12,000 men, the Allied death toll was nearly 20,000. The five week campaign cost fewer than 400 aircraft for the destruction or capture of 1,850 enemy machines. Some important lessons were also learned about joint operations.

THE INVASION OF ITALY

On July 24, 1943, Mussolini was dismissed from office by King Victor Emmanuel III after a vote of no-confidence in him in the Fascist Grand Council. He was placed under house arrest. Intelligence reports indicated to the Allied leaders that the Italians would soon desert their ally, Germany. Negotiations centred on this possibility delayed plans for the invasion of Italy. Meanwhile, the Germans poured men and equipment into the Italian peninsula, but the initiative had been lost to the Allies and that was to cost the Germans dearly. On September 12, when the Allies had already invaded Italy, Mussolini was rescued from captivity in a daring airborne commando raid and was taken to

Germany. Afterwards, Hitler set up a new Fascist state, the Salò Republic, with Mussolini, now a puppet, at its head, and its headquarters at Gargagno on Lake Garda.

On September 3, the Eighth Army finally crossed the Straits of Messina under massive air cover and made unopposed landings at Taranto. In marked contrast, the amphibious assault on Salerno by the US Fifth Army nearly proved disastrous. The German defenders were easily able to predict the landing sites and the 16 divisions under the American General Mark Clark had to fight long and hard to establish a beachhead. The British plan was to drive through Calabria and link up with Clark, trapping the Germans in the process. The skill and ferocity of the German defenders forced the Allies to rethink, and enabled Field Marshal Albert Kesselring's forces to escape the pincer movement.

Numerical superiority and command of the skies again proved the greatest asset as the Allies slowly advanced north. To aid the advance the "cab rank" system was pioneered, whereby standing patrols of ground attack aircraft could be called down by radio to strike at targets by ground forces with the shortest possible delay. Naples fell on October 1, and airbases at Foggia were in Allied hands by October 5. These were the two prime Allied objectives, as the latter brought the Romanian oilfields within striking range of nine squadrons of No 205 Group, which commenced operations in April 1944.

As the Allies continued their drive north on either side of the Appenine Mountains, and with winter rapidly approaching, Kesselring formed a defensive line, the "Gustav" line, stretching across the peninsula from the Liri Valley to the approaches to Rome.

With hopes of an early victory dashed, the Allied commanders decided to focus on the capture of Rome. The elaborate and imposing Gustav line stood directly in their path, persuading the Allies to embark on an amphibious assault behind the line at Anzio. Operation Shingle, as the assault was code-named, was nothing short of a disaster.

Although an attack on the Gustav line at Cassino diverted some of Kesselring's forces, General Clark failed to consolidate the beachhead after an almost unopposed landing on January 22. A rapid German counter-attack nearly drove the US Sixth Corps back into the sea. For the next four months, the American forces were subjected to intense bombardment and attack and fought a bitter defensive battle against the German 14th Army.

On the Gustav line, a renewed offensive along the line, code-named Operation Diadem, began on May 11. Twelve Allied divisions were opposed by six German divisions. On the west coast, the corridor through Cassino allowed General Clark to advance on Rome. Clark ignored General Harold Alexander's order to cut the German retreat, allowing them to escape again. On June 5, the day before the Allied landings in Normandy, northern France, Rome fell to the Allies. The Germans once again stabilised a defensive line across the peninsula as their troops were diverted to Normandy in droves. The line was drawn from La Spezia to Pesaro, and as the winter of 1944–5 drew in, there was a lull in operations. The fighting in northern France had shifted the focus of Allied and German strategy. In the spring of 1945, the US Fifth Army and British Eighth Army, 17 divisions in all, launched a final attack along the Senio River, some 32km (20 miles) south-east of Bologna. Massive aerial bombardment of the German forward divisions and their reinforcements had weakened their defences, and they crumbled in the face of the advance. Throughout the following week, Allied aircraft systematically destroyed bridges across the Po River, so denying the Germans any possibility of retreat. The surrender of General Heinrich von Vietinghoffs Army Group C on May 2, 1945, brought to an end the bitterly contested and costly Italian campaign.

BELOW: A Supermarine Spitfire Mk Vc taxies to the runway on a captured airfield near Naples. The ungainly, but clearly vital, tropical air filter is fitted over the engine air intake.

CHAPTER 5

HITTING BACK

Until the spring of 1941 defensive commitments dominated RAF operations in Europe, but the escalating threat from the U-boat packs in the Atlantic soon brought the role of Coastal Command to the fore. From mid-1943 Bomber Command unleashed its rebuilt force on Germany.

Writing after the War, Winston Churchill revealed that, of all aspects of the hostilities, the losses sustained by the North Atlantic convoys caused him most concern. The task of protecting these convoys, on which Britain's survival depended, became the single highest priority for Royal Air Force Coastal Command and may be seen as its most important contribution to the War. The relative ineffectiveness of

ABOVE: A Hurricat-equipped merchantman. This device was designed specifically to counter the Luftwaffe's Fw 200 Condor maritime bomber. After catapulting from the prow and = fighting off the attacker, the pilot was required to ditch alongside.

LEFT: Bomber Command crews catch a few moments of relaxation before preparing for the night's attack.

Bomber Command operations in the early stages of the War, albeit in the face of many obstacles, was a similar cause for concern, and was offset only by the the tenacity and bravery of the aircrews. With effective equipment and organisation, by 1944 the RAF bomber fleets were already delivering devastating blows against Germany's ability to wage war.

COASTAL COMMAND

Few flying boats of any ability, or land-based aircraft with suitable range for the demands of maritime operations, were available to the RAF at the outbreak of war. The warnings of World War I, when German U-boats wreaked havoc on British shipping, had not, apparently, registered with its commanders. Coastal Command was the most neglected of all RAF commands, perhaps because of the prewar antipathy between the Royal Navy and the RAF. The most capable aircraft on the inventory of Coastal Command, which had been formed in 1936 from a number of disparate units, was the Avro Anson. Soon after war broke out, British merchant shipping crossing the North Atlantic from Canada came under attack from the new, highly effective U-boats operating in the Atlantic Gap, the long stretch of their voyage where no air cover was available. Allied losses during the first six months of the War were appallingly high. The Royal Navy was fully occupied in the Mediterranean and could spare few destroyers for escort duties, and not many of these were equipped with radar. By the end of 1940, the Ansons had been gradually phased out of service by the Lockheed Hudson, a military version of the Lockheed 188A airliner with heavier armament and twice the range. At this time, Coastal Command squadrons also began to take delivery of Beaufort torpedo bombers to supplement the increasing numbers of Sunderlands, Whitleys and Wellingtons on Coastal Command strength. The Beaufort proved highly

BELOW: A photograph from an RAF Liberator that has just straddled a U-boat with a stick of depth charges. AA gunners can be seen in the conning tower. The boat sank 13 minutes later.

effective in the anti-shipping role, particularly against Axis convoys in the Mediterranean.

RADAR

The equipment that revolutionised the war at sea was undoubtedly radar. During the Battle of Britain it had proved a vital asset, and when the first Air to Surface Vessel (ASV) sets were made available to Coastal Command in 1941 results began to improve even further. In addition, the anti-submarine bombs that had proved so ineffective against U-boats in the early stages of the war were also gradually replaced by a new and powerful depth charge. But these were dark days for Coastal Command. They had sunk only two U-boats and the toll on merchant shipping convoys began to escalate to unsustainable levels during the summer of 1941. Even so, some notable victories were scored – particularly the attacks on the German battleship Gneisenau and cruiser Lützow by torpedo-carrying Beauforts, which badly damaged the former vessel and put the other out of commission.

Coastal Command strength was boosted by the arrival of new aircraft later in 1941, the most important of them being the American long-range Consolidated PBY Catalina and Liberator designs. The total number of aircraft stood at 633

Coming to this Theatre shortly...

"TARGET for TO-NIGHT"

The film that tells you about the Service which needs you.

JOIN THE R·A·F·
OR THE W·A·A·F·

ABOVE: An advertisement for a wartime propaganda film about the Royal Air Force. Such films did much to glamourise the dangerous job of Bomber Command crews.

by the end of 1941. In February of the next year, however, the Command received a very public setback when a substantial German fleet that included the German battlecruisers *Scharnhorst* and *Gneisenau* left Brest and, after slipping through the English Channel, escaped to home waters. During the course of the year, increasing commitments in the Mediterranean and Far East resulted in the re-deployment of all the Beaufort squadrons to these theatres, so depleting the strength of the home force, which for a time had to rely on unsuitable Handley Page Hampdens for anti-shipping work.

A significant innovation in the battle against the submarines was pioneered from June, 1942. U-boats recharging their batteries on the surface under the cloak of darkness were difficult to spot, even with radar. By equipping maritime patrol aircraft with a powerful spotlight that could illuminate the target after radar acquisition, the hunters became the hunted.

Consequently, in the next twelve months, until June 1943, Coastal Command sank 71 U-boats. At about the same time, a Strategic Bombing Offensive by Bomber Command began to take effect. The RAF were aided in this theatre of war by British Intelligence, whose interpretations of German Enigma radio traffic became increasingly accurate and allowed U-boat

movements to be plotted. Rocket-firing Beaufighters also began to make their mark on Axis coastal shipping in the latter part of 1943, in both the north European and Mediterranean theatres.

As mentioned in the preceding chapter, Coastal Command units operating in the Mediterranean theatre were instrumental in denying Rommel the vital supply route from southern Italy. By the autumn of 1943, it was clear that the German shipyards could no longer keep pace with the rate of losses the Allies were inflicting on them. The first Strike Wing, consisting of one anti-flak squadron and a torpedo-carrying squadron, had been formed in November 1942 and the effectiveness of this unit prompted the formation of another five by June 1944.

Although German radar counter-measures were constantly improving, advances in Allied radar science allowed Coastal Command to maintain its lead in the anti-submarine war This was furthered by Portugal's decision to allow the Azores, 1126km (700 miles) out in the Atlantic, to be used as a base for Coastal Command operations from October 1942. The move by Britain's oldest ally proved to be a major factor in the battle, since it allowed for additional coverage of the Atlantic shipping lanes. Subsequently, between July 1943 and D-Day, Coastal Command sank 114 U-boats. Although the German navy was able to increase U-boat production, the loss of experienced crews was far outstripping the rate at which they could be trained. The volume of men and material brought to Britain during preparations for D-Day shows that there was a dramatic reversal in fortunes in the Battle of the Atlantic.

BOMBER COMMAND

As we have seen, an unswerving, but mistaken, faith in the primacy of strategic bombing in air operations had existed in the RAF during much of the 1930s and contributed to the poor air defence and maritime patrol capabilities of the Service. In fact Bomber Command had entered the war as the strongest of the three home commands, with an operational strength amounting to 325 aircraft; the total strength was closer to 952, but 17 squadrons were withdrawn to form Operational Training Units and a further 10 were sent to France in 1940. The aircraft were a mixture of Wellingtons, Whitleys, Battles, Blenheims and Hampdens.

The terrible losses sustained during the Battle for France have already been recounted. During the Battle of Britain that followed, operations were focused on selected German industrial targets and on the ports and airfields preparing for the invasion. Here, Bomber Command was able to make a significant contribution, sinking many of the invasion barges in their harbours during repeated attacks. This was done despite the inadequacy of the aircraft in service. Strategic attacks began on the night of May 15/16, 1940, and continued until the final surrender of Nazi Germany on May 8, 1945. German industrial targets in the Ruhr, Münster and

Cologne were attacked without significant success, primarily because of poor navigational aids and inadequate weather intelligence. At this time, aircraft carried out their own navigation plotting.

There were, however, no specialist navigators in the crews and unless the aircraft could be flown with great precision and the target was not covered by the thick cloud that often blanketed the Ruhr, then accuracy was often very poor. From October 1940 Britain was released from the threat of invasion and Bomber Command was able to concentrate on the strategic bombing campaign that had been vigorously championed by many senior officers. However, RAF commanders remained overly optimistic about the damage these raids were causing to German industry, despite clear evidence to the contrary, which was provided by the pilots and interpreters of the RAF Photo Reconnaissance Unit.

VICKERS WELLINGTON

The Wellington was a prewar design, and shouldered much of the burden of the early bombing campaign. The innovative geodetic airframe designed by Barnes Wallis enabled the Wellington to absorb a great deal of damage. Total production of this outstanding aircraft amounted to 11,461.

ABOVE: An RAF pilot, shot down over Germany, is laid to rest with honours by members of the Luftwaffe, a gesture of respect that was abandoned as the bombing of German cities intensified.

In one notable report from the Photographic Interpretation Section on raids against two synthetic oil plants at Gelsenkirchen, it was shown that in almost 300 sorties no major damage had been caused. Yet despite this, and further evidence provided by the PRU, the chief of Bomber Command, Air Marshal Sir Richard Pierse, held firm to the belief that targeting these oil facilities should form the focus for the RAF bomber squadrons through the winter of 1940 and early spring of 1941.

THE SUBMARINE THREAT

Because of the increasing threat presented by U-boats operating from Lorient, St-Nazaire and Bordeaux, in March 1941 Winston Churchill instigated a directive ordering Bomber Command to concentrate on reducing this threat by bombing the bases and the shipyards in Kiel, Bremen and Hamburg. This saw the start of a shift towards area targeting that was to develop over the next four months. During this period, a total of 12,721 sorties were flown against these and other targets, for a loss of 321 aircraft, yet no appreciable impact was made on submarine operations. After the fall of France in June 1940, the Germans had lost no time in French Atlantic ports and these proved resistant to RAF bombing. By

July, though, the threat to the Atlantic sea route had receded somewhat, and Bomber Command was free to return to the strategic bombing campaign again. Significantly, another Directive, dated July 9, turned attention to the dislocation of the German transportation systems and to destroying the morale of the population as a whole and of industrial workers in particular.

However, in the following months both navigation and bombing accuracy within the Command were again shown to be hopelessly inadequate. An analysis of 100 raids carried out in June and July 1941 showed that only one crew in four had reached the target and bombed within 8km (5 miles) of it. The position did not improve during the autumn and after a disastrous raid on November 7/8, when only 48 out of the 169 aircraft dispatched against Berlin reached the target, and four of these attacking aircraft were lost, Pierse was summoned to the Prime Minister's country base at Chequers in Buckinghamshire to answer some searching questions. The result was that operations against Berlin were suspended, and Bomber Command retired to lick its wounds and re-equip

ABOVE: Boisterous bomber crews are driven to their aircraft dispersal areas before a raid on Berlin in 1944. Most bomber crew members were sergeant rank.

BELOW: An aerial reconnaissance photograph showing the devastation suffered by the city of Cologne as a result of the Strategic Bombing Offensive.

with new navigation and bombing aids in preparation for a fresh strategic bombing offensive planned for 1942.

THE STRATEGIC BOMBING OFFENSIVE

In the winter of 1941, the Air Staff drew up a new plan for attacking 43 of the main industrial centres in Germany, with a fleet bolstered by a sizeable US strategic bomber force based in Britain. In February, an important change was made in RAF policy. The concept of bombing specific industrial targets was abandoned in favour of area bombing, and henceforth the primary objective would be the morale of the civilian population. In the Directive much emphasis was attached to the new Gee navigational aid, which relied on pulsed transmissions from ground stations in Britain. The transmissions were interpreted in the air through a cathode ray tube, and this allowed the pilots to guide aircraft to their targets. Although the first equipment was crude and not especially accurate, it was the first of four important systems used during the course of the War.

In February 1942, Pierse was replaced in command by the man whose name became, and remains, synonymous with Bomber Command – Air Chief Marshal Sir Arthur Harris. Harris has attracted considerable controversy for his dogged

BELOW: Air Chief Marshal Sir Arthur Harris (fourth from left, seated) assesses the effect of Bomber Command raids on the German war machine. In truth their effect was very limited.

AIR MARSHAL SIR ARTHUR HARRIS

Harris is perhaps the best-known and most controversial of RAF commanders. He was an enthusiastic advocate of strategic bombing throughout his career, but provoked a storm of controversy over indiscriminate assaults on German cities. Harris was often at odds with Portal, the RAF Chief of Staff, yet was held in great regard by the men of Bomber Command.

and unflinching belief in area bombing, but his dynamic personality and an iron determination made him a hero among his men. Morale in the Command had been sapped by constant criticism, and Harris played an important part in reviving flagging confidence.

During the spring, massed raids were undertaken against German cities. These caused widespread destruction and death among the civilian population, culminating in the first Thousand Bomber Raid against Cologne at the end of May, which resulted in immense damage. Harris countered his critics with the sentiment that the German people "have sown the wind and will now reap the whirlwind".

In August, Sir Charles Portal, Chief of the Air Staff, ordered that a special Pathfinder unit should be raised to further boost bombing accuracy. This would be made up of the

best crews and charged with finding and marking the target with flares as a guide to the main fleet. Although strongly resisted by Harris, the unit was created under Gp Cpt Donald Bennett and began assembling at their newly-assigned bases on the same day B-17s of the US Eighth Army Air Force carried out their first attacks.

PATHFINDERS

The concept of the Pathfinder Force was simple. Bombing accuracy, even with Gee equipment, was far below the level required and it was clear that another method was needed. The Pathfinder Force (PFF) was established from Nos 7, 35, 83, 109 and 156 Squadrons, flying a mixture of Halifaxes, Stirlings and Wellingtons. This force eventually became No 8 Group. The first operation was not a success. The target, Flensburg on the Baltic coast, was not hit at all, but during the autumn results began to improve with the introduction of specially designed incendiary marking devices. In the latter part of the year an improved navigational aid, code-named Oboe, began to equip PFF Mosquitoes. These light, fast and high-flying aircraft were the ideal tool for the Oboe equipment, which had a strictly limited range and could control only a single aircraft to the target at any one time. Oboe was used exclusively by PFF Mosquitoes until the end of the War.

ABOVE: The de havilland Mosquito was the most capable RAF light bomber of the war. Here a Mk IV of No 139 Squadron receives a load of 225-kg (500-lb) bombs in February 1943.

H2S

From January 1943, a device came into service that was to prove an asset to Bomber Command. This was the H2S equipment, a primitive ground-mapping radar which, with skilled operation, could be used to distinguish targets on the ground. Most importantly, it enabled aircraft to bomb through cloud, was self-contained and so could be carried by all aircraft, did not rely on ground stations, and could not be jammed by the enemy. The Luftwaffe responded to this new threat with their own innovations. Their night fighter force was equipped with efficient airborne radar by mid-1942 and took an increasingly heavy toll of Bomber Command. In response, British scientists developed Window, an early form of chaff consisting of strips of aluminium metallic foil to confuse German ground radar operators.

On the night of May 16/17, 1943, the legendary Dambusters raid was undertaken by specially trained crews of 617 Squadron flying Lancaster bombers, each carrying the bouncing bomb devised by Barnes Wallis, the designer of the Wellington. Both the Möhne and Eder dams were breached and extensive damage was caused to industry in the Ruhr. Although the extent of this damage was exaggerated at the

time, and one of the dams targeted, the Sorpe, escaped, the raid was an undoubted boost to morale.

THE HAMBURG RAIDS

At the end of July 1943, Hamburg was subjected to the most devastating attacks of the war so far. By night massed formations of Bomber Command aircraft utilising Window and guided by PFF aircraft equipped with H2S attacked Germany's second city. During the day the US Eighth Army Air Force dispatched more. A huge firestorm created by a raid on 27/28 July killed some 41,800 people , injured 38,000 more, and prompted a mass exodus from the city of 1,200,000 others. These combined attacks against German cities continued throughout the summer and were supplemented by raids on northern Italy by Bomber Command aircraft in early August. The damage inflicted during these raids was undoubtedly a factor in the decision of the Italians to agree an armistice with the Allies on September 8. Ten days later a massed attack by 596 Bomber Command aircraft hammered the German missile-producing facility at Peenemünde on the Baltic coast, causing substantial damage and generating crucial delays in the V2 project. The efficiency of the German defences, particularly the night-fighter units, cost some 40 aircraft

PREPARATIONS FOR THE SECOND FRONT

With planning for the invasion of Europe well under way, the Allied Expeditionary Air Force was created in November 1943 under Air Marshal Trafford Leigh-Mallory. This included No 2 Group, which had left Bomber Command on

ABOVE: A rare wartime colour image of RAF Lancasters in flight. The aircraft are on the strength of No 50 Squadron and the date is August 28, 1942.

AVRO LANCASTER

The Lancaster was without doubt the finest heavy bomber in British service during World War II. Four Merlin engines provided significantly improved performance over previous types, coupled with useful defensive arma- ment and offensive load. Lancasters took part in every major night attack on Germany, and carried a bigger load of heavier bombs than any other aircraft in the European theatre. Introduced into service in September 1941, Lancasters soon showed their superiority by dropping 132 tons of bombs for every aircraft lost.

June 1 to form part of the 2nd Tactical Air Force. The man chosen as deputy leader of this vast aerial task force, which also included the US Ninth Army Air Force and the whole of Fighter Command, was desert veteran Air Chief Marshal Sir Arthur Tedder. Harris was fully aware that he would be required to sacrifice more aircraft to this cause, as would the US Eighth Army Air Force.

During the winter, both Wellington and Stirling bombers were withdrawn to less demanding roles in the face of mounting losses to the German defenders. The Luftwaffe crews were aided by some important electronic innovations. One of these was a device code-named Naxos, which allowed the fighters to home in on British H2S transmis- sions. Harris ordered a partial H2S silence for October, and a tail warning device was introduced on British aircraft. Unknown to the British, however, this equipment acted like

DAMBUSTERS

From Enemy Coast Ahead, *the account of the Dambusters raid by its leader, Wing-Commander Guy Gibson:*

"The gunners had seen us coming. They could see us coming with our spotlights on for about miles away. Now they opened up and their tracers began swirling around us; some were even bouncing off the smooth surface of the lake. This was a horrible moment: we were being dragged along at four miles a minute, almost against our will, towards the things we were going to destroy. I think at that moment the boys did not want to go. I did not want to go. I thought to myself, in another minute we shall all be dead."

The RAF raids on Hamburg infuriated the German Führer. At a conference on July 25, 1943 he stated: "Terror can only be broken by terror! Everything else is nonsense. The British will only be halted when their own cities are destroyed. I can only win the war by dealing out more destruction to the enemy than he does to us. In all epochs that has been the case, and it is just the same in the air. Otherwise our people will turn mad, and in the course of time lose all confidence in the Luftwaffe. Even now it is not fully doing its job …"

LEFT: One of the Dambusters' modified Lancasters with Barnes Wallis' "bouncing bomb" held in the cradle. The gear and chain spun the device to the optimum rotational speed before release.

its knees remains undisputed. Production in some sectors of industry actually increased. But by diverting valuable forces away from the front into defence during this period, Bomber Command not only gave indirect and vital support to the Red Army at a crucial stage in the conflict in Russia but, more important, helped prepare for the Second Front the Russians so badly needed.

a beacon to guide the enemy into the attack. Despite the heavy losses of the autumn and the forced withdrawal of nearly one third of his fleet by January 1944, Harris remained convinced that strategic bombing held the key to victory and pressed on with attacks on Berlin through the winter. The losses sustained during these attacks were quite insupportable; from November 1943 to March 1944 a total of 587 aircraft were lost, almost all of them Lancasters. The Battle of Berlin failed to deliver the final victory Harris had promised and was considered by many a resounding defeat for the Allies. The success of the Strategic Bombing Offensive is often judged in the simple terms of its prewar aims, and the fact that German industry was not brought to

RIGHT: Members of Guy Gibson's crew are debriefed after the Dams raid by an intelligence officer (with glasses). Harris is standing behind him.

CHAPTER 6

THE PATH TO VICTORY

In the final year of the war the RAF played a vital role in the success of the Normandy landings and the subsequent campaign in North-West Europe. In the Far East the RAF toiled with heat and a determined enemy to finally wrest conquered British territories from the Japanese occupiers.

In 1944-5, the final year of the war, the RAF provided decisive tactical and strategic support to the ground forces in their drive through north-west Europe to Berlin and victory. Meanwhile, on the other side of the world, the men of the RAF South East Asia Command battled through to retake Burma and Singapore. From December 1941, and for three months after the victory in Europe on May 8, 1945, they

ABOVE: RAF ground crew manhandle 27-kg (60-lb) HE rocket projectiles at an airbase in southern England duirng the June 1944 Normandy campaign. The Typhoon/rocket combination proved to be deadly against ground targets.

LEFT: A Hawker Typhoon is prepared for its next close-support mission at a forward airfield in France.

fought in the so-called "Forgotten War" to defend India against a ferocious, committed and often ruthless Japanese enemy. In addition, they relieved the occupied territories of Singapore and Malaysia, and helped to deliver the final victory in August 1945.

OVERLORD AND BODYGUARD

The plan for the Normandy invasion was accepted by the end of the 1943 and the code-name Operation Overlord was chosen. General Bernard Montgomery was selected as operational commander. Elaborate deception plans were formulated, code-named Bodyguard, which leaked false information that the invasion would go in at Calais. In reality a massive invasion force was gathering in southern England for a projected assault on five beaches west of the Orne River

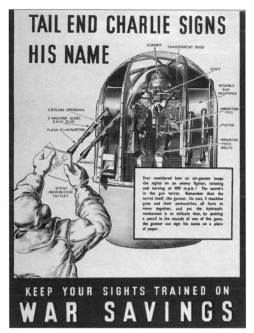

Despite the losses of the spring, by June 1944 RAF Bomber Command had 1408 bombers, and 4102 other types in readiness for the invasion. The Americans contributed at least as many again. Control of this daunting aerial armada, including Bomber Command, had passed to General Eisenhower in mid-April in order to simplify the chain of command. Although Bomber Command continued to attack German cities in the late spring, most RAF effort was concentrated into attacks on transportation centres in France so as to hinder enemy movement after the Normandy landings. To maintain the secrecy surrounding the Overlord, simultaneous raids were carried out throughout northern France, particularly in the Pas de Calais region. From the end of May, the heavily fortified defensive positions forming the Atlantic Wall were targeted , and once again, so as to conceal the intended invasion area, the sites attacked stretched right along the coast.

In the hours prior to the invasion on June 6, Bomber Command flew 1200 sorties against enemy targets and in the hours after the first troops had landed, its crews flew more than 1000 further sorties, dropping over 5000 tonnes of bombs on enemy communications, airfields and ports. In the Straits of Dover a unit of 617 Squadron dropped Window to confuse the enemy radar sites, while 406 RAF transport aircraft dropped airborne forces behind the Normandy beaches. These units drew two attacking Panzer divisions into the battle and these were subjected to heavy fire from close support aircraft of the Tactical Air Force.

At the same time, British and Canadian troops were storming ashore on Gold, Juno and Sword beaches, supported by a massive naval bombardment and heavy bombing attacks. The landings on the British beaches met with only light

near Caen – codenamed Sword, Juno, Gold, Omaha and Utah. The force, comprising nearly 3 million men was to be supported by massive strategic and tactical air support. Air superiority was a vital part of the Allied plan, and Eisenhower decided to delay the invasion by one month to further reduce the operational strength of the Luftwaffe.

Despite its later fame, The Hawker Typhoon made an inauspicious operational debut. as an interceptor in 1941. The Napier Sabre 1 engine was not fully developed, the aircraft performed badly at high altitudes and had a slow rate of climb. An improved Sabre engine and a switch to low-level operations saw the Typhoon finally come into its own.

resistance. By the evening of June 6, all 150,000 men of the invasion fleet were ashore and beachheads had been established. Air attacks continued to harry the German divisions in the week after the landings and the Allied advance from the beachheads continued apace.

CLOSE AIR SUPPORT

With the bridgehead in Normandy secured, Allied tactical aircraft were deployed to operate strips built by airfield construction units. By June 27 there were 38 Allied fighter and fighter-bomber squadrons operating from 13 improvised airfields. While the fighter squadrons maintained air superiority over the battlefields, the fighter bomber squadrons were used in the close air support role, a vital feature of the campaign through north-west Europe.

In September 1939, the RAF had possessed virtually no dedicated close air support aircraft that could destroy German armour. The importance of tactical close air support was realised by Air Marshal Tedder during the campaign in North Africa. Cooperation between Tedder's Desert Air Force and Montgomery's Eighth Army worked effectively in this theatre because the air commander retained full control of his subordinate units, and could respond to various threats as he saw fit.

The role of dedicated RAF close air support squadrons, equipped predominantly with aircraft such as the Hawker Typhoon, was to provide ground forces with a form of aerial artillery to suppress German defences. Field-based ground-to-air radio links meant that attacks could be called in on

*ABOVE: **Hamilcar gliders (centre) and Halifax towing aircraft lined up and waiting for the order to begin the invasion of France.***

targets at short notice. During the battle for France, aircraft armed with armour-piercing rockets and cannon were used to cripple German supply columns and columns of armour.

BREAKOUT

American forces captured the port of Cherbourg on June 26, and by July 1 the Allies had equalled the German forces in strength. With nearly one million men and 177,000 vehicles opposing him, Adolf Hitler persisted in refusing to allow divisions in the Pas de Calais region to move south. Eisenhower seized this opportunity to break out from the beachhead and between July 7 and July 15 six massive carpet-bombing raids were carried out in front of the Allied

HAWKER TYPHOON

Although originally conceived as a fighter, the Typhoon offered only limited performance at altitude and was better employed as a ground attack aircraft. This solid and stable aircraft was an excellent weapons platform and perhaps the finest close air support aircraft of the War. Rocket-firing Typhoons made a decisive impact during the Normandy campaign, notably against German armour at the Falaise pocket.

positions at Normandy. These attacks wreaked considerable destruction on the German troops, but also caused casualties among the Allied forces.

General Bradley's 1st Army divisions achieved a vital breakout to Avranches on July 31 and secured the Cotentin Peninsula. On August 15, with the Allied breakout in full flood, an Allied attack was launched between Cannes and Toulon, throwing the German defences into further confusion. Sixteen German divisions of Army Group B were trapped in a pocket around Falaise between the advancing Allied armies, and were virtually annihilated by rocket-firing Typhoons of 2TAF in one of the most brutal displays of air power witnessed in the War. At the same time, a bombing offensive was launched against ports along the Channel coast, where isolated German garrisons were holding out. The ports were heavily damaged, and civilian casualties were high. Bomber Command alone flew nearly 6,000 sorties against them, losing only 14 aircraft in the process.

THE ROCKETS

On June 13, 1944, Hitler launched the first ten of his reprisal weapon, the V-1 flying bomb, at London. The offensive grew in intensity, reaching a total of 800 in the first week of July. Half of RAF Bomber Command strength was diverted to attack the launching sites along the coast of Europe, and air defences were reorganised along the south coast to intercept the missiles. With a top speed approaching 645 km/h (400 mph), only the latest generation of Allied fighters, including the Spitfire Mk XIV, Mustang III and Tempest V could intercept the flying bombs. The Gloster Meteor, the first RAF jet aircraft, was first used in operations against the V-1 in July 1944. A massive air offensive against the production lines failed to halt production of the V-1 or the V-2 ballistic missile. This latter weapon, which flew through the stratosphere, could not be intercepted and it struck its target without warning, but of the 10,492 V-1s launched against London and the Channel ports between June and the end of the war the RAF claimed 1,847 shot down.

In mid-August the German Armies tried to consolidate their positions on the River Seine, but in the face of overwhelming Allied air superiority, they were forced to fall back. The rapid advance had left Allied supply lines overstretched, however, and the armies were still reliant on the temporary harbour in Normandy. To keep the RAF tactical air squadrons in the front line required considerable support from 46 anti-aircraft, rifle and armoured car squadrons of the RAF Regiment. The logistical problems that arose because of the rapid advance caused a significant loss of momentum, giving the Germans time to consolidate their defences.

FOLLY AT ARNHEM

Eisenhower's wish to speed the Allied advance lay behind his support for Montgomery's disastrous airborne assault at Arnhem. Operation Market Garden, as it was code-named, was designed to capture three important Dutch river positions. The attack was launched on September 17 and was supported by a force of 1,240 fighters and 1,113 bombers, but rapidly ran into considerable opposition from two SS Panzer divisions. The airlift of reinforcements was hampered by bad weather and even when the transport aircraft were able to take off, they failed to rendez-vous with the fighter escort and suffered heavy losses. After six days, 57 aircraft had been lost and the inadequacy of RAF transport support was fully exposed, though through no fault of its own. Only

LEFT: An aircraft of the Tactical Air Force pulls up after attacking a railway line with rockets. One of the salvos has scored a direct hit on the line.

ABOVE: A dramatic overhead shot of a Spitfire and V-1 bomb in close formation. The RAF pilot is about to "tip over" the German bomb with his wingtip, a technique pioneered in 1944.

2,000 of the 9,000 British airborne troops survived this badly conceived, ambitious and ultimately expensive operation.

As autumn began to descend on western Europe, the Nazi position was becoming increasingly untenable. Hitler's armies were fighting in northern and southern France, in northern Italy, and on the vast eastern front in Russia. And yet the winter of 1944–5 would prove that the Germans were not yet prepared to accept the defeat that was nevertheless inevitable. Hitler had correctly presumed that the twin drive by Montgomery's 21st Army Group and Bradley's 12th Army Group had seriously overstretched Allied supply lines, which were still dependent on the artificial harbours at Normandy. All through the autumn, tough German resistance impeded rapid Allied advance on all fronts, yet south of the Ardennes forest the 6th Army Group made great gains and the Americans were at the west bank of the Rhine by December.

THE BATTLE OF THE BULGE

During late November, 25 German divisions, virtually all of them reserve troops, were assembled for an attack through the heavily-wooded, semi-mountainous Ardennes region that lay at the centre of the Allied line. Hitler aimed to punch through this line, split the British and American forces, and stabilise the Western front. Even at this stage, and without being aware of the Allied commitment to Germany's total defeat, Hitler believed the British and Americans would

sue for peace. On December 16, the German units, which included 11 Panzer divisions, attacked through the Ardennes, achieving complete surprise. They rapidly overran the six US divisions guarding a 97-km (60-mile) front and began the race to Antwerp. Eisenhower was slow to react and snowstorms grounded the Allied air forces.

The German forces made speedy advances but were plagued by the problem that had hampered their operations for months – shortage of fuel. The 6th Panzer Army came close to capturing the massive fuel dump south of Spa, but were driven back. A rapid reinforcement of 200,000 men was rushed into the battle. On December 23 the weather cleared and the tactical air units were able to fly 600 missions in support of the ground operations. Attacks on the German armour, and assaults by US 1st and 3rd Armies, forced the Germans onto their back heel. By the end of the year the Germans were in retreat through the forest, and by the end

THE ROYAL AIR FORCE REGIMENT

The Royal Air Force Regiment was established in the early 1920s and during the inter-war period served on many overseas deployments. During World War II the main task of the Regiment was airfield defence. After the invasion of France in 1944 no fewer than 46 Regiment squadrons were deployed to secure Allied airfields, 19 of them anti-aircraft units, 21 of them rifle squadrons, and six equipped with armoured cars.

ABOVE: An aerial photograph taken during the attack on the battleship Tirpitz in Tromso Fjord on November 12, 1944. The German seamen threw up a thick smoke screen over the target.

of January 1945 all the German gains made during the Ardennes offensive were back under Allied control.

On New Year's Day 1945, the RAF received an expensive warning against complacency when the airfields of 2TAF were attacked by a fleet of 800 German aircraft. Some 144 Allied aircraft were destroyed on the ground, but the aircrew losses suffered by the Luftwaffe effectively ruled them out of further air operations.

Bomber Command resumed the air offensive again on August 15, 1944 and was released from the control of Supreme Headquarters in mid-September. The Air Staff were divided over the choice of target systems to be attacked, but in the event a Directive of September 25, 1944, prioritised the German petroleum industry. In mid-October, massive attacks were launched against Cologne and Duisberg and with Allied air superiority virtually unchallenged, losses were

very low. Bomber Command had by this time reached a strength of 94 squadrons.

The closing months of the War saw a continuation of numerous and widely scattered attacks across Germany and the remaining occupied territories. Two particular operations were notable. The first was the sinking of the battleship Tirpitz in Tromso Fjord by Nos 9 and 617 Squadron on November 12, 1944. The vessel was struck by at least two 5500-kg) 12,000-lb Tallboy bombs before rolling over. Second was the controversial attack on Dresden on the night of February 13/14, 1945. This city had escaped heavy bombing thus far in the War, and the Air Staff suggested it as a target in a letter to Harris dated January 25, 1945. The raid was carried out by a force of 773 Lancasters in two waves, which dropped more than 1,800 tons of bombs. A massive firestorm similar to that seen at Hamburg engulfed the old city, killing as many as 50,000 people and destroying many of its historic buildings. The last major bombing operation of the War was concentrated against the naval base at Kiel on May 2/3.

THE FALL OF GERMANY

In the spring of 1945, as the bulk of the Allied forces returned to the offensive, Hitler continued to refuse to allow Field Marshal Karl von Runstedt to order a withdrawal behind the Rhine. Montgomery planned a set-piece assault across the river, code-named Operation Plunder, for March 24. In this context, it was important that effective air preparation and support was organised, and through the night prior to the assault, heavy bombing attacks were concentrated on bridges, railway centres, airfields and barracks. Early the next morning, aircraft and gliders of Nos 38 and 46 Groups, RAF Transport Command, mounted their assault across the river. Soon after a unit of the US 1st Army had brilliantly snatched

---

THE BATTLE OF BERLIN

An extract from the official British history of The Strategic Bombing Offensive against Germany:
"Bomber Command was compelled, largely by German night-fighter force, to draw away from its primary target, Berlin, to disperse its effort and to pursue its operations by apparently less efficient means than hitherto. The Battle of Berlin was more than a failure. It was a defeat."

*ABOVE: **Japanese infantry make their way through the wreckage of a downed RAF Harvard during the capture of a British air base at Tabo, Borneo, 1942.***

the Remagen bridge over the Rhine, Patton sneaked a unit of the 3rd Army across the river at Oppenheim. Effective German resistance ended after the Allies crossed the Rhine and advances were rapid.

The Luftwaffe was by now reduced to cursory attacks, primarily because of a chronic shortage of fuel, enabling Allied aircraft to operate with impunity over Berlin. The Reichstag was stormed by Russian troops on April 30, the same day Adolf Hitler committed suicide. On May 2, with the position now hopeless, General Helmuth Weidling, the Commandant of Berlin, called on his troops to lay down their arms.

WAR IN THE FAR EAST

Singapore was selected as the main British base in the Far East in the early 1920s, and its defence was planned to depend upon coastal batteries and torpedo bombers. The aircraft chosen for this were Vickers Vildebeest bi-planes, which were operated alongside No 205 Squadron, which had Shorts Singapore flying boats.

In July, 1940 it was realised that the defence of the base at Singapore would depend entirely on air power, and that to protect all British interests in the area would require a force of some 566 aircraft. The modest force at Singapore was strengthened with Blenheims, Hudsons and Catalinas, but when the Japanese attack was launched on December 8, 1941, RAF strength across the whole region amounted to only 326 aircraft.

In Malaya, these aircraft were operated from 22 airstrips, but all of them were poorly protected and only a handful were surfaced. The needs of communication and early warning were also poorly served.

THE FALL OF SINGAPORE

Only two hours after the attack on the US fleet at Pearl Harbour, Hawaii, on December 7, 1941, forces commanded by Lieutenant-General Tomoyuki Yamashita battled their way ashore at Kota Bahru and Patani, on the north-eastern coast of Malaya. The invasion fleet was spotted 483km (300 miles) offshore by a Hudson of No 1 Squadron RAAF and was attacked with vigour during the landings. The only type of fighter aircraft available to the defenders were four squadrons of Brewster Buffaloes, aircraft that had been rejected by the RAF as inadequate for the European theatre. Against the agile Mitsubishi A6M Zero it proved equally unsuited. Many Buffaloes were destroyed on the ground during Japanese bombing attacks and yet more aircraft were lost in daylight raids on Japanese airfields. Yamashita's forces proceeded to drive down the coastal plain on the west of Singapore island at a stunning pace, with the Commonwealth forces in headlong flight before them.

On December 10, the British suffered a devastating loss when the ships of Force Z, the battleship *Prince of Wales* and the battle cruiser *Repulse* were sunk by Japanese aircraft while sailing north to harass the invasion fleet. As a result of confusion between Air Vice-Marshal Pulford and Acting Admiral Sir Tom Phillips, the fleet commander, the two Royal Navy vessels had not been provided with air cover, although it has to be said that neither officer was mistaken in his actions.

With this disaster, the British were dealt a lesson about the importance of air cover for modern naval forces.

By January 10, 1942, Kuala Lumpur was in Japanese hands and 17 days later Lieutenant-General Arthur Percival, commander of the Commonwealth forces, ordered a withdrawal to Singapore. Reinforcements for the final defence of Singapore included a small number of Hurricane fighters that had begun to arrive on Christmas Day, 1941, and these were able to put up a more effective defence when unescorted Japanese aircraft bombed Singapore Island on January 20. On the following day, however, the raiders returned with an escort of Zero fighters and five Hurricanes were lost. By the end of January virtually all the aircraft had been evacuated, with the intention of continuing the fight from Sumatra, across the Strait of Malacca.

The assault on Singapore began on February 7 and on February 15, Percival surrendered the garrison of 80,000 men to Yamashita. It was, in Churchill's words, "one of the greatest disasters in British military history", and it had taken a mere 70 days. The RAF set up its headquarters at Palembang on Sumatra, but this too was abandoned in the face of overwhelming odds on February 18. By June 1942, the Philippines, Burma, Malaya, Hong Kong and the Dutch East

BELOW: Three RAF P-47 Thunderbolts returning from an attack temporarily halt the activity on the squadron flight line at a forward airbase on the Arakan front in Burma, December 1944.

Indies (Indonesia) were occupied by Japanese forces. In the first six months of its Pacific campaign, Japan had established a defensive island barrier around the Pacific Basin and captured crucial raw materials from those islands.

THE BURMA CAMPAIGN

Burma formed part of Britain's extensive colonial territories in South-East Asia, and was thus a likely target for the expansionist policy of the Japanese. On December 11, 1941, 35,000 men of the Japanese 15th Army crossed the border from China. Their primary objective was to halt the flow of arms along the Burma Road to the Kuomintang, the forces led by the Nationalist Chinese leader General Chiang Kai-shek. They were opposed by a slender, inadequately trained and poorly equipped British force, supported by perhaps 30 aircraft of US Major General Claire L Chennault's Flying Tigers volunteer force and an RAF squadron with 16 Buffaloes on its strength. Air attacks on the Burmese capital, Rangoon, began on 23 December. A squadron of Blenheims arrived on January 7, followed by 30 Hurricanes. These aircraft acquitted themselves well, but in the following months the Japanese advanced steadily north, taking Pegu on March 4, before launching an assault on Rangoon. Despite the presence of the very capable General Harold Alexander, Rangoon was abandoned on March 6. The remaining RAF and American units pulled back to Lashio, a vital staging point on the Burma Road, and were subjected to heavy

ABOVE: Orde Wingate's Chindit guerillas offloading supplies from an RAF Transport Command Dakota at a location behind enemy lines. Supplies were more often para-dropped.

bombardment at the base. By April 30, Lashio had been captured, although some RAF personnel were evacuated to India by Dakotas. Pursued by the Japanese forces, the British made a long retreat back to India, and at the end of May, Burma was in Japanese hands. The monsoon season then enveloped the region, affording the British a vital respite to build up their forces for the expected Japanese attack on India.

At this stage of the War, Burma was a low priority in comparison to the European and Mediterranean theatres. Under Air Marshal Sir Richard Pierse, who had arrived in March 1942 to take over command of the RAF forces, the Service's strength in India was rapidly built up in the summer to 26 squadrons. These aircraft were used in support of a limited counter-offensive on the Arakan coast in December, which had the primary aim of capturing the port of Aryab. The operation was an unmitigated disaster, and for the next two years the Allies had to satisfy themselves with the small scale successes of Brigadier Orde Wingate's Chindit guerrillas. An interesting aspect of this operation, which lasted between February and May 1943, was that Wingate's forces depended entirely on air resupply by two squadrons of RAF Dakotas.

Part of the reason for the reluctance to launch a counter-offensive during this two-year period was that an air link across the Himalayas had already ensured that supplies were still reaching the Chinese and the Allies were reluctant to commit forces to the area. South-East Asia Command was formed under Lord Mountbatten in November 1943, and by early in the following year this had expanded to include 48 RAF and 17 USAAF squadrons, based at a complex of 275 new airfields protected by a radar network.

These aircraft proved a vital asset when on February 3,

1944, the Japanese 28th Army attacked the southern sector of the Indian frontier, with the object of capturing Kohima and Imphal. RAF Dakotas brought vital supplies to the defenders of these towns while Allied aircraft strafed the Japanese attackers. The strengthened 15th Corps under the British General Slim met the attack and forced the 28th Army to begin withdrawing three weeks later. Further attacks in the central and northern areas of the frontier proved both unsuccessful and costly for the Japanese; when they began a general withdrawal on July 4, only 30,000 of the attackers remained.

Stubborn Japanese defence hampered the Allied attempts to recapture Burma, but with a force amounting to some 90 RAF and and USAAF squadrons, against which the Japanese could pit only 125 aircraft, Slim possessed an overwhelming advantage. Allied troops continued their advance south with overwhelming air support and on November 19 and December 3, 1944, the British 14th Army had crossed the Chindwin river at two separate points. By March 1945, they were on the outskirts of Mandalay. Remorseless attacks on enemy supply dumps preceded the advance and when the capture of Wanting by Chinese forces in January 1945 permitted the reopening of the Burma Road, victory was more or less assured. On May 3, a combined airborne and amphibious attack was launched to retake Rangoon. Effective Japanese resistance ended within a week.

BELOW: Spitfires of No 136 Squadron flying low over a dispersal area, signifying the destruction of Japanese aircraft.

CHAPTER 7

THE UNEASY PEACE

As peace again descended over Europe, a new threat to Western security emerged in the shape of the Warsaw Pact. Defending Britain and her NATO allies from this threat was the primary role of the RAF during the nuclear age.

During World War II, the RAF had grown into a vast global organisation with over 1 million personnel and 55,000 aircraft. Victory and the peace that followed saw a reduction in that strength, but with the Cold War and new battle lines drawn between East and West, the RAF faced a new responsibility for nuclear deterrence and remained in the front line of the Cold War for 40 years.

In the two years after the War, Government defence strategists tried to absorb the implications of peace and the

ABOVE: Construction workers toil to extend the runway at Gatow airfield in Berlin during the Berlin airlift, while an Avro York taxis behind.

LEFT: An overhead shot of an RAF Boeing E-3 Sentry Airborne Early Warning Aircraft. The Sentry is operated by Nos 8 and 23 Squadrons and is a vital part of Britain's air defence network.

emergence of atomic weapons. The Defence White Paper of 1947 accepted the need to reduce the Service in terms of personnel and equipment, but highlighted the importance of preserving its structure and continuity. Defence planners subsequently proposed a force that would, ideally, hold 1,500 aircraft in 147 squadrons. In the face of the harsh economic climate then prevailing, the Labour government's Cabinet projected its own view that Britain was unlikely to find herself involved in conflict in the immediate future, and the proposed force was excessively large.

By June 1948, the RAF possessed a front line strength in aircraft that was only about half the size suggested by the Air Staff. The outflow of personnel from the Service had created a dearth of qualified technicians for the new and increasingly complex aircraft then coming into service, and this required comprehensive restructuring in the training and organisation of the technical branches. In general, though, in these early

THE BERLIN AIRLIFT

One of clearest indications of the growing divide between East and West after the end of World War II in Europe came on June 24, 1948, when the Soviet Union imposed a blockade on all road, rail and canal links from the Western Zones of Occupation into West Berlin. The RAF and USAAF responded quickly to the blockade and within four days Avro York and Dakota aircraft of Transport Command were airlifting supplies to the beleaguered West Berliners. Supplies were flown into Gatow and Tempelhof airfields, and by Sunderland flying boats to the Havelsee. At the height of the airlift in April 1949 some 8,000 tons of food and fuel were delivered every day. The Soviet blockade was lifted on May 12, 1949, by which time the RAF had flown over 19 million km (12 million miles) and carried some 300,000 tonnes of freight to the city.

years of peace, there was a lack of modernisation throughout the Service.

A LOST OPPORTUNITY

In the 1930s, a young RAF officer named Frank Whittle conducted pioneering research into jet propulsion and by mid-1944 the RAF possessed an operational jet aircraft, the Gloster Meteor. The revolutionary aspect of this machine was its powerplant, though the design and construction techniques employed on the airframe were wholly conventional. Research into high-speed flight proved the limitations of these techniques, particularly the unswept wing, and it became clear that a radical new approach to aircraft design was needed before the potential of jet propulsion could be fully realised.

For a decade after the War, the RAF persevered with obsolescent straight-winged designs such as the Meteor, the de Havilland Vampire and the de Havilland Venom. America and the USSR wasted no time in swept-wing supersonic research. The MiG-15 first flew in 1947, powered by an jet engine supplied by the British, and during the Korean War of 1950–3, these aircraft proved devastating in air-to-air combat against Meteors of the Royal Australian Air Force. In the light of this reality, with no other aircraft available to replace them and with little Government stimulus for the aviation industry, the RAF

RIGHT: Refuelling a Gloster Meteor fighter. The Meteor formed the backbone of Britain's air defence for nearly a decade, from 1945-55.

was faced with little other choice. The only really effective fighter aircraft ordered in this period, in 1951, was the Hawker Hunter.

The RAF also faced the challenge of replacing the antiquated air defence network, and its reorganisation is a key feature of this period. The old Chain Home sites were progressively updated with modern American radar. Six air defence sectors were created to cover the whole of Britain, each with a Sector Controller. Close control of the actual interception was the responsibility of radar-equipped Ground Controlled Intercept stations.

STANDOFF – THE RAF ENTERS THE COLD WAR

The assumptions of the 1947 Defence White Paper proved to be short-sighted. In April 1949, against a background of increasing hostility between Allied and Soviet forces in Central Europe, which culminated in the Berlin Airlift, Britain became a founder member of the North Atlantic Treaty Organisation. These new international alignments prompted a steady programme of rearmament and retraining within the RAF that doubled the strength of Fighter Command by 1951. The RAF received Boeing B-29 bombers under the US Mutual Defence Assistance Program. Two key motives lay behind the escalation of the arms race. The first was a growing realisation in the West that the Soviet Union possessed modern weapons technology, a fact indicated by the atomic test carried out by that country in 1949 and by the appearance of the MiG-15 fighter aircraft. Second, Soviet involvement in the Korean War was perceived by many Western military analysts as the first step towards world Communist domination.

During the early 1950s, NATO forces in Central Europe were steadily increased to counter this perceived threat. Although it was known that the Soviets were rapidly expanding their intercontinental bomber fleet at this time, a conventional attack could not be discounted. It was widely accepted that this would involve a massive thrust across the

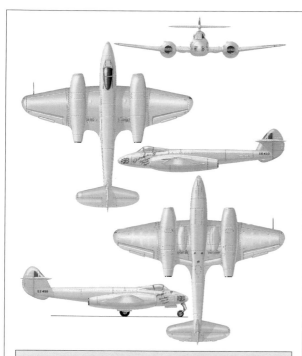

On November 7, 1945, this Gloster Meteor MK IV piloted by Group Captain H J Wilson raised the absolute speed record to 975.6 km/h (605.8 mph). In September 1946 the aircraft was flown to 990.8 km/h (615.3 mph). The Meteor equipped RAF front line fighter units well into the 1950s, despite the obsolescence of the straight-wing design.

Central European Plain. Containing the threat from Soviet strategic bomber fleets, and their conventional forces on the Central Front, was the dominant influence on RAF doctrine and equipment procurement for 40 years.

THE SECOND TACTICAL AIR FORCE

In the Western zones of occupation the 2nd Tactical Air Force was expanded to 50 squadrons by 1953. Under the terms of the NATO agreement, command of RAF forces in Germany was assigned to the Supreme Allied Commander, Europe, in the event of a war. When Canberra bombers began to enter RAF service in 1952, it was also understood that although most squadrons were home-based, they would be available for NATO operations in the event of a crisis. The Canberra was designed as a high level bomber that could deliver conventional weapons, thus making it an ideal aircraft for operations on the Central Front. In the mid-1950s the growing threat of Soviet surface-to-air missiles led to the

deployment of a low-level interdiction version of the aircraft that could carry tactical nuclear weapons.

The prohibitive cost of expansion forced the Conservative government elected in October 1951 into some retrenchment. The concept of expanding conventional forces seemed to many a pointless expense in view of the atomic weapons possessed by the Soviet Union. In 1952 the Global Strategic Paper effectively substituted strategic nuclear deterrence for conventional forces. The V-bomber force under development was expected to fulfil this new strategy, and at a much reduced cost. Expansion of the Second Tactical Air Force was streamlined in line with these plans, reaching a peak strength of 35 squadrons by the end of 1955. In that same year, the first Hawker Hunters F Mk 4 fighter-bombers arrived in Germany.

From 1955, Fighter Command also re-equipped with the Hunter, one of the most impressive post-war British aircraft. At the end of 1956, its front-line strength stood at 33 squadrons, 16 with the Hunter, one with the new Gloster Javelin and the rest soldiering on with Venoms and Meteors.

THE 1957 WHITE PAPER

In 1957, a comprehensive and now notorious Defence White Paper was issued under Defence Minister Duncan Sandys that had a very profound and essentially negative impact on the Royal Air Force. First, it stressed the importance of the V-bomber Force then entering service to the nuclear deterrent Britain had decided to adopt in the early 1950s. It then outlined plans to supplement this Force with American Thor ballistic

DE HAVILLAND VAMPIRE

The Vampire was the first jet ground attack aircraft to enter service with the Royal Air Force. Its design was fairly conventional, but it became a popular aircraft with pilots because of the good visibility afforded by the cockpit position and its outstanding manoeuvrability. By January 1952, 13 of the 16 RAF squadrons in Germany were equipped with these aircraft, and others were deployed in the Middle and Far East. The Vampire was also used in the day fighter role. The FB.5 had a top speed of 869 km/h (540 mph) at 6096m (20,000ft) and a ferry range of over 1127km (700 miles)

been laid for a stand-off delivery nuclear system. This evolved into the Blue Steel missile programme. The plan had been to equip an element of the V-Force with the American Skybolt ASM, in exchange for submarine facilities in Scotland, but the programme ran into serious development problems, and after successful trails with Blue Steel, this weapon was accepted in December 1962. Five squadrons were eventually equipped with the weapon. It was powered by an extremely volatile liquid propellant and in service took up to two hours to load onto an aircraft.

TWILIGHT OF THE V-FORCE

It was inevitable that at some time the effectiveness of the high-flying strategic bomber would be undermined by Soviet rocket technology. In 1963, the American government agreed to sell Polaris missiles to Britain to equip submarines that would eventually take over the British nuclear deterrent role. Until that time, the V-Force would remain in the front line, although its aircraft were reconfigured for low-level penetration under enemy radar. The Vulcan and Victor crews were also trained in QRA (Quick Reaction Alert) procedure and assigned to NATO. This ensured that one crew from every squadron was always at 15 minutes' readiness to strike.

missiles, which would be sited in Britain. The last and most controversial assumption made by the Paper was that although defence of the bomber airfields was an essential task, surface-to-air missiles would eventually replace fighter aircraft in this role.

THE V-FORCE

In 1946, the Air Ministry had issued Specification B35/46 detailing a requirement for a long-range bomber to replace the current fleet. It was assumed that the future target would be the Soviet Union and therefore the aircraft would need to possess long range and a weapons-carrying capability in excess of 4536kg (10,000lb).

After submission of proposals from a number of manufacturers, the Avro, Handley Page and Vickers designs were chosen for development. The least radical of the designs, the Vickers Valiant, entered service in August 1954. Although this aircraft did not fully meet the Specification, it provided a useful intermediary until the delivery of the new V-bombers and conducted all the British trials with atomic weapons. In February 1957, the radical delta-wing Avro Vulcan entered service, followed in November by the distinctive crescent-winged Handley Page Victor.

Between 1957 and 1969, the RAF V-Force formed the basis of national defence planning for Britain. All its aircraft were painted in a distinctive overall white paint scheme, and the crews were subject to a rigorous selection procedure. Many Valiants were subsequently converted into tankers to support the V-Force, and both the Vulcan and the Victor received uprated engines in due course. By 1962, the force stood at 18 squadrons, all of them based in Britain.

BLUE STEEL

The Air Ministry had realised that Soviet air defences would become increasingly capable and in the late 1950s plans had

---

HAWKER HUNTER

The Hunter is fondly remembered by a whole generation of RAF pilots as a superbly agile fighter with useful ground-attack capability, and is undoubtedly the most successful British post-war aircraft. It was powered by a single Rolls-Royce Avon turbojet engine. Piloted by Neville Duke, the one-off Mark 3 gained the world speed record at 1171 km/h (727.6 mph). The Hunter remained in production for 13 years, with total output reaching 1985 aircraft.

From Neville Duke's Book of Flight *(Cassell, 1958):*
"I opened up the throttle, accelerating quickly at full power to maximum level speed, and did a partial roll into a dive about forty degrees from the horizontal. Speed built up quickly. The Mach meter needle swung round to 0.95, the buffet and vibration seemed to strike with extra violence, but they were short and sharp-lived. The next day I repeated the run and this time aimed the dive at Dunsfold Aerodrome. In the cockpit I could see or hear nothing myself, but over the r/t came the message: 'Two bangs received, loud and clear.' The Hunter was definitely supersonic."

From 1964, the V-Force was gradually run down. In 1964, a serious structural weakness in the wing main spar of a Valiant tanker prompted the RAF to scrap the whole fleet. The air-to-air refuelling role was taken over by converted Victor aircraft, which in any case had proved unsuitable for low level operations. It had been expected that Polaris submarines would spell the end for RAF strategic bombers at the end of the 1960s, but the Vulcan soldiered on. The Vulcan bombers assigned to the V-Force were converted to optimise them for the low-level tactical strike role previously filled by the Canberra, which served in this capacity until 1983.

STRUCTURAL CHANGES

In the mid-1960s the Soviet Union achieved parity with the US in terms of its nuclear arsenal and thereafter a form of strategic nuclear balance began to develop. Soviet conventional forces were perceived as the primary threat and RAF forces were restructured and re-equipped in response. Responsibility for the nuclear deterrent was transferred to the Royal Navy in the late 1960s and greater emphasis was once again placed on conventional forces. Some major restructuring in the organisational structure of the Serivce was undertaken during this period. In 1968, Bomber Command and Fighter Command, and later Coastal and Signals Commands, were merged to form Strike Command. This was divided into six Groups and was supported by a new Air Support Command containing the transport squadrons. In line with the growing Soviet submarine threat, the anti-submarine capability of the RAF was increased and

TORNADO

In the mid-1960s, it was realised that the cancellation of the TSR.2 programme would create a large gap in RAF strike/attack capability, and that interim aircraft such as the McDonnell Phantom and Blackburn Buccanneer did not have the development potential to meet future demands in this role, or in that of air defence. At the same time, however, it was understood that with acceptable variations, the strike/attack and interceptor roles could be filled by the same aircraft. An international consortium, Panavia, was set up to design and produce the aircraft. The development of this project was a daunting task, but nonetheless, the first of 229 Interdictor/Strike (Gr Mk 1) aircraft for the RAF were delivered in 1991, followed by 165 of the Air Defence Variant.

the role of the V-Force was expanded to include low-level tactical strikes.

NEW AIRCRAFT

As well as the V-bombers, a large number of new aircraft were brought into service. The venerable Blackburn Beverly was retired in 1968 and was replaced by the Lockheed Hercules C.Mk 1, which to this day is one of the best used and most valuable of RAF aircraft. In the strategic transport role, the de Havilland Comet and Bristol Britannia were sup-

No. 29 Squadron at RAF Collingsby became the first front-line user of the Tornado ADV, becoming operational on 1 November 1987. In the NATO structure it is declared to SACLANT (Supreme Allied Commander Atlantic), and has a maritime air-defence commitment.

*RIGHT: **Bloodhound air-to-surface missiles on their launchers at RAF Watton. This was the type of missile that Duncan Sandys had predicted would replace the manned interceptor aircraft.***

plemented by Vickers VC-10s and Short Belfast in 1966. Both were very capable machines. Although the 10-strong Belfast fleet fell victim to defence cuts in 1976, the VC-10 will remain in service well into the 21st century. Helicopters were used by the RAF as early as 1948. The first really effective transport helicopter in RAF service was the Westland Wessex, which entered service in 1964. But neither this aircraft nor the Bristol Belevedere had a useful heavy lift capability and the latter machine was withdrawn in 1969. This left a very real gap, which was filled only by the arrival in RAF service of the Boeing-Vertol Chinook in 1982.

One of the great disasters to befall the service in the 1966 defence cuts was the cancellation of the TSR.2 project. This tactical strike aircraft was developed from 1958 to replace the Canberra and showed great potential in the early stages of flight testing. With two other expensive developments programmes for the RAF underway at this time, the burden on the budget was deemed too great by the Labour government and all three projects were cancelled. As a result of this decision, the RAF bought the Blackburn Buccaneer, an aircraft originally designed for carrier-borne operations. Although it was much ridiculed at the time by sceptics within the RAF, in service the Buccaneer proved a great success, notably during the 1991 Gulf War.

The growth of the Soviet nuclear-missile carrying submarine fleet in the 1960s led to a parallel expansion in RAF anti-submarine capability. From 1970, the ageing fleet of piston-engine Avro Shackleton aircraft that had served in this role were replaced by the Nimrod, a much modified version of the de Havilland Comet jetliner.

AIR DEFENCE

One of the clear aims of the 1957 Defence White Paper was the replacement of fighter aircraft for airfield defence with surface-to-air missiles. This process began with the deployment of 352 Bloodhound missile systems between 1958 and 1961, during which time Fighter Command was reduced in strength from 600 aircraft to 140. It was fortunate for the survival of the air defence network that the English Electric Lightning arrived in service in this period. This impressive interceptor aircraft had twice the speed of its predecessors and a phenomenal rate of climb. The first aircraft was delivered in 1959, and apart from a poor range, which was never really resolved on subsequent variants, the Lightning proved an exceptionally fine interceptor in service.

From 1969, the Lightning was supplemented and slowly replaced in service by the McDonnell Phantom. The RAF purchased this American-built aircraft, but only on the insistence of the Government that the aircraft be powered by Rolls-Royce Spey engines. The RAF received an initial 48

FG.1 interceptor aircraft, and these were supplemented from July 1974 by ground-attack FGR.1 aircraft; these were transferred from squadrons after delivery of the SEPECAT Jaguar.

From the late 1960s, the main task for the air-defence squadrons was intercepting Soviet long-range bombers and reconnaissance aircraft, such as the Tupolev Tu-95 Bear, which were sent to probe the northern reaches of the air defence network over the North Sea. It was also recognised that Soviet bombers had the potential for launching considerable numbers of surface-to-air cruise missiles from points far to the north-west of the British Isles, and therefore long-range interception of these aircraft became a priority.

TACTICAL SUPPORT

The expansion of the tactical force was a clear indication of changing strategy within NATO. When Air Support Command was set up in 1967, it inherited the tactical transport and ground attack aircraft of No 38 Group. This was equipped with two squadrons of Hunter FGA Mk 9s. These were supplemented, and subsequently replaced, by Phantom FGR.Mk 1s and also by the Hawker Siddeley Harrier from July 1969. The Harrier was a significant addition to the tactical capabilities of the RAF. Vertical/Short Take-Off and Landing capability (V/STOL) allowed the Harrier to operate away from airfields with self-contained support units. Although the first Gr.1 Harrier had a limited payload/range parameter, the aircraft proved an asset to NATO forces.

From March 1970, the RAF built up a sizeable fleet of 165 single-seat and 35 two-seat versions of SEPECAT Jaguar aircraft, an Anglo-French strike/attack aircraft that had excellent low-level performance and a useful weapons load. The Jaguar gradually assumed the role formerly filled by the FGR Mk 2 Phantom. Air Support Command had been absorbed into Strike Command in 1972, and the whole of the Jaguar force eventually came under its command.

The fourth TSR.2, XR222, which would have flown in June 1965 had the programme continued. The main landing gear is shown, complete with rear damper struts, which were never flown. Note the tabbed "tailerons", the first to fly as primary roll-control surfaces (except for the air-launched X-15) and the one-piece slab vertical tail.

THE RAF IN GERMANY

The considerable cost of setting up the V-Force at the end of the 1950s made it inevitable that the size of the RAF presence in Germany would be reduced. In 1959, the 2nd Tactical Air Force was renamed RAF Germany and by 1961 six front-line squadrons had been disbanded. Westland Wessexes of No 18 squadron joined the Command in 1965, and the following year, the Gloster Javelin squadrons were re-equipped with Lightning interceptors. In conjunction with the re-equipment programme throughout Strike Command, RAF Germany received Phantom, Harrier and Buccaneer aircraft.

By the end of 1972, the Command was made up of eight fixed wing and one rotary wing squadrons. Improvements were made from the mid-1970s to the airfield facilities, including Rapier surface-to-air missile batteries and Hardened Aircraft Shelters. As Jaguar became available, Phantom squadrons Nos 14 ,17, 31 and 32 transferred their aircraft to interceptor units. In 1980 tactical support for No 1 BR Corps was improved by the introduction of the Aérospatiale SA 330 Puma. These were supplemented in 1983 by the Chinooks of No 18 Squadron. In September of that year, the first Tornado aircraft arrived at No XV Squadron. This aircraft was to spend the last days of the Cold War with front-line squadrons in Germany.

THE END OF THE COLD WAR

Signs of a new warming in East/West relations began to appear after 1985, following the appointment in that year of Mikhail Gorbachev to the Soviet Presidency. Defence spending had become an unsustainable burden on the Soviet economy, and one of the steps taken by Gorbachev was to seek an end to East/West hostility. This manifested itself in a number of ways. The most important was a gradual withdrawal of Soviet forces in Central Europe, and then a succession of popular revolutions in former Warsaw Pact countries.

By early 1990, the Royal Air Force had reached the final stages of a major re-equipment programme that had seen the Phantom and Buccaneer replaced by Tornado. A massive leap forward in airborne Early Warning capability had been realised with the replacement of Avro Shackletons by Boeing E-3 Sentry aircraft, and in the training role, the Jet Provost was succeeded by the Shorts Tucano. The diminished threat from the Eastern Bloc had in turn led to a reduction in the numbers of air defence aircraft.

BELOW: Tornado F-3s formate with a venerable Avro Shackleton and, in the background, the aircraft that replaced it—the Boeing E-3 Sentry.

CHAPTER 8

WITHDRAWAL FROM EMPIRE

In the post-war years the RAF was involved in all the major counter insurgency operations in former British colonies, and in the early 1980s was called upon to provide support in the campaign to retake the Falkland Islands.

From 1948 to 1960. the RAF was involved in three major campaigns of counter-insurgency: Malaya (1948–60), Kenya (1952–60) and Cyprus (1955–9). In 1956, following Egyptian nationalisation of the Suez Canal, Britain was drawn into a short but politically damaging campaign in

ABOVE: A Westland Whirlwind of No 155 Squadron, RAF, disembarking men of the RAF Regiment (Malaya) in Selangor State, Malaya, April 1957. The RAF pioneered the use of helicopters for troop insertion and resupply in this theatre.

LEFT: Supplies are dropped from a Vickers Valetta to troops in Malaya. Such drops were a vital part of RAF air support duties.

Egypt, which had a far reaching impact on future RAF commitments. During the decade that followed, economic, political and military pressures forced successive British governments to conduct a process of withdrawal from colonies across the globe.

The transition to self-rule was far from trouble-free and was marked by conflict in Borneo (1962–6) and Aden (1963–7). Each of these campaigns was a considerable commitment and a major strain on British resources, in turn spurring further withdrawals. By the end of the decade, Britain had granted independence to almost all its former colonies. During the relative peace of the 1970s, NATO commitments drew much on RAF resources. However, the

The Canberra is an aircraft that first flew in 1949 and, since that date, aircraft of 12 different marks have been exported to 11 air forces worldwide. The most numeous of these was the Canberra B2, of which over 400 were manufactured.

1982 Falklands War in the South Atlantic proved that the RAF still had the capability to mount a successful campaign in a distant outpost of the once far-flung Empire. Since then, in the 1990s, RAF overseas forces, most notably in the Arabian Gulf and Balkans, have been concerned with implementing Britain's role as international policeman.

MALAYA

In June 1948, after months of civil unrest and acts of terrorism by the Malayan People's Communist Party, the Malayan High Commissioner declared a state of emergency. When the state of emergency was declared, the RAF presence in Malaya amounted to eight squadrons, distributed among the airfields at Changi, Seletar and Tengah in Singapore and Kuala Lumpur in the north. The activities of the terrorists were widely dispersed, preventing effective attack operations. RAF participation during the first 18 months of the campaign were therefore restricted to photo-reconnaissance by de Havilland Mosquito Mk 34s, and air re-supply of police and troop units operating in the jungle. From 1949, Bristol Brigands were used for low-level ground attack. Flying conditions in Malaya were never less than challenging – the jungle canopy covering 80 percent of the peninsula hid the enemy, weather conditions were hazardous and aircraft had to operate far away from servicing and supply bases.

By 1950, the number of RAF aircraft in Malaya had risen to 160, with 36 in reserve. Later that year, Hawker Tempest, de Havilland Hornet and Short Sunderland squadrons were detached to Malaya, followed in December by the first jet aircraft to be employed during the emergency – the de Havilland Vampire. The superb field of vision available from the cockpit made this aircraft a firm favourite among RAF

pilots in Malaya. In keeping with the process of re-equipment during the early 1950s, aircraft of World War II vintage were gradually replaced. The three squadrons of Douglas Dakota transports received Vickers Valletta C.Mk 1 and Gloster Meteor Mk 10s, which were eventually superseded by the Supermarine Spitfire Mk 19 in the PR role.

From February 1953, the helicopter force in Malaya was gradually built up, initially with Sikorsky S-55 and then later with Westland Whirlwind aircraft. The use of helicopters transformed the Malayan campaign by providing greatly improved flexibility of air support through the use of roughly-cleared strips in the jungle. RAF activity peaked in 1954, with some 14 squadrons in theatre. Through the late 1950s, responsibility for military security in Malaya was increasingly shared with the Royal Australian Air Force, the Royal New Zealand Air Force and the Malayan Air Force. RAF strength was gradually reduced until 1960, when the emergency was formally ended.

KENYA

The use of aircraft proved a equally decisive factor in the three-year campaign against nationalist insurgent elements in the British crown colony of Kenya between 1952 and 1955. In 1952, a state of emergency was declared after an uprising of Mau-Mau rebels. In April 1953, the RAF committed 12 North American Harvard trainers to operate as ground-attack aircraft; within a year these had flown more than 2000 sorties. In November 1953, Avro Lincoln bombers of No 49 Squadron began a three-month detachment. These were used for widespread bombing of terrorist areas and, as in Malaya, this tactic proved more effective than point attacks by de Havilland Vampire jet fighters. Ground support was undertaken by Vickers Valettas, Hunting Pembrokes, Auster observation aircraft and Bristol Sycamore helicopters.

The Mau-Mau were a poorly equipped though organised enemy. Once again, intelligent harmonisation of air and ground forces brought a successful conclusion to the campaign in 1955.

CYPRUS

With the deteriorating situation in the Middle East after 1945, the importance of Cyprus as a military base increased. In July 1954, the British government announced that Cyprus would not be granted independence, provoking Greek Cypriot leader Archbishop Makarios III to form an underground military force called EOKA (National Organisation of Cypriot Struggle). The withdrawal of British forces from

*RIGHT: **Blackburn Beverely transport aircraft at a rough airstrip in the Radfan mountain region in Aden, where most of the campaign against the rebels was fought.***

Suez led to increased dependence on the RAF airfields at Nicosia and Akrotiri, but the deployment of British reinforcements at these bases was seen as a further provocation by the Greek nationalists. RAF helicopters, notably the Bristol Sycamore, again provided support during operations against EOKA terrorist bases in the Troödos Mountains, which increased in intensity after the declaration of a state of emergency in November 1955. Avro Shackletons from Malta were engaged in surveillance patrols to prevent smuggling of arms.

A negotiated settlement between all three factions was reached in 1959, and today the RAF continues to maintain Akrotiri as an operational unit. The strategic importance of the base was highlighted during the 1991 Gulf War, when it was used as a major staging point for Operation Granby, the air war in that conflict.

The practical knowledge gained by the RAF in the Malayan, Kenya and Cyprus campaigns was to prove useful as the withdrawal from empire gathered pace in the 1960s, and during operations in Northern Ireland.

SUEZ – THE WATERSHED

Indian independence in 1947 destroyed at a stroke the raison d'être for maintaining a British presence in Egypt, Sudan, Libya, Transjordan, Aden and Somaliland, where demands for military withdrawal had been escalating since 1946.

In April 1954, Colonel Gamal Abdul Nasser came to power as a result of a bloodless coup, and an agreement for the withdrawal of British troops was signed on November 19, on the understanding that British troops would be moved back in should the freedom of the Canal be threatened.

However, Nasser's support for Arab nationalist movements, his opposition to the Jewish state of Israel, increasingly strong ties with the communist Eastern Bloc, and, finally, his seizure of the Canal on July 26, 1956 and the nationalisation of the Suez Canal Company, provoked Britain, France and Israel to attack Egypt in October 1956.

With much of its strength already committed in Malaya, Kenya and Cyprus, the RAF had limited resources for Operation Musketeer in Egypt. Seventeen squadrons of English Electric Canberra and Vickers Valiant bombers were assembled at Malta and Cyprus, supported by de Havilland Venom, Hawker Hunter and Gloster Meteor fighters. The Egyptian Air Force was equipped with Soviet-supplied MiG-15 and -17s, which were in many respects superior to the Venom and Meteor. On October 31, three waves of RAF Canberra and Valiant bombers from Malta and Cyprus bombed Egyptian airfields from high altitude, but destroyed only 14 aircraft on the ground in the face of light opposition.

Throughout the next day, land and carrier-based aircraft attacked every Egyptian Air Force base west of Sinai, but again these attacks had only limited effect, as most of the

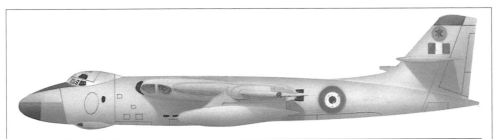

The Vickers Type 667 Valiant was one of the first of a new generation of postwar, long-range bombers developed to allow Britain to maintain a viable nuclear bomber force. It first entered service in 1955. It was used to deploy high-explosive bombs during the Suez campaign of late 1956.

ABOVE: A thick pall of smoke rises from the oil tanks hit during the initial raids by RAF bomber aircraft on Port Said, Egypt.

Egyptian aircraft had been moved to safety. On November 1, carrier-based ground-attack aircraft were committed to the battle. Daylight and night raids over the following 72 hours virtually eliminated the EAF, with 50 aircraft destroyed and a further 40 damaged, with no British or French losses.

Early on November 5, a battalion of British troops emplaned at Cyprus onto 26 RAF Vickers Valletta and Handley Page Hastings transports. Protected by fighters and ground-attack aircraft, the force was successfully dropped onto Gamil airfield at 0515 hours. Within 30 minutes, the objective was in British hands and the Paras began their push to Port Said at the northern end of the Canal. Less than 24 hours later, a seaborne assault on Port Said began, preceded by intensive air strikes against Egyptian defensive positions. The assault was a resounding success and rapid advances were made during the day toward the next objective, Ismalia. However, American fears of Soviet intervention, coupled with domestic pressures, forced Britain and France to accept a ceasefire agreement, which came into effect at midnight. During the entire campaign, a total of 260 Egyptian aircraft had been destroyed, for the loss of one French and five British aircraft.

Despite its undoubted success as a military operation, the Suez affair provided irrevocable proof that, with dwindling economic and military resources, Britain could not afford to maintain her imperial overseas commitments.

BORNEO

For the British government, the most favourable means of disposing of the colonies that made up British Borneo – Sarawak, Brunei and Sabah, was through the creation of the Malaysian Federation under Tunku (Prince) Abdul Rahman, son of a Sultan of the state of Kedah. The Indonesian

president, Achmed Sukarno, regarded this as a threat to his plans for a greater Indonesia, and sought to destroy the idea.

In April 1963, Sukarno launched a cross-border offensive against isolated police and army bases. Major General Walker, the British commnder, faced immense difficulties in preventing incursions across the 1500-km (932-mile) long border. His slender force was considerably bolstered by the arrival of twin-rotor Bristol Belvederes in May. These were used alongside the Blackburn Beverleys, Scottish Aviation Pioneers and Bristol Sycamores already in theatre for the purpose of airlifting troops and supplies. Surveillance work undertaken by RAF Shackleton and Canberra crews was thus essential to identify crossing points and tracks in the jungle. Equally important was the task of resupplying forward bases near to the border, something which could often be accomplished only by air. To provide a secure operational base for the RAF the airfield was developed on the island of Labuan.

From September 1963, the rebel campaign intensified and a well-defined pattern of air supply began to emerge. Helicopters were used for a growing number of tasks – medevac, troop lifting and rotation, and the lifting of heavy equipment. The RAF also sent conventionally armed elements of the V-bomber force to Borneo to engage in bombing operations against Indonesian infiltrators.

In December 1963, Sukarno committed regular Indonesian forces to the battle. Hostile incursions by Indonesian aircraft led in February 1964 to the establishment of an air defence zone along the border, policed by Hawker Hunter and Gloster Javelin fighters. This was later extended to cover all Malaysian airspace, but fleeting attacks by Indonesian aircraft on border villages continued to be a problem for the RAF. During the first six months of 1965, the Indonesians made 40 attempted landings by sea and air. In response to this increasing aggression, Malaysian air defences were considerably strengthened by the Javelins of No 64 Squadron and the surface-to-air missiles of No 65 (SAM) Squadron.

By the end of the year, the Indonesian campaign had lost momentum, and control of the frontier was ceded to the Commonwealth and Malaysian forces. A peace agreement was reached in August 1966.

BOEING-VERTOL CHINOOK

The heavy-lift capability of the Royal Air Force was greatly boosted by the introduction of the twin-rotor Boeing-Vertol Chinook in August 1980. The Chinook can accommodate up to 45 fully-equipped troops or a variety of other loads up to a maximum of 10 tonnes. Fitted with internal fuel tanks for long-range ferry deployments, the Chinook has a range of 1609km (1000 miles). The aircraft saw action in the Falklands in 1982 and in the 1991 Gulf War.

ADEN

By the time Britain was withdrawing her forces from Sarawak and Sabah in September 1966, Khormaksar in Aden was the sole remaining RAF base in Arabia and was in the throes of an insurgency. In 1964, the year after Aden had joined the Federation, Britain stated its intent to retain the territory as a naval and air base. This provoked conflict with Egyptian-backed urban terrorists and Yemeni guerrillas in the mountainous Radfan region of the country. Although it was predominantly an Army operation, the campaign against these insurgents relied heavily on RAF support for resupply and troop movement and logistical support. Pioneer, Twin, Beverley, Andover, Argosy and Pembroke transport aircraft were all employed in theatre in support of ground forces, supplemented by Wessex and Belvedere helicopters. Hunter fighter and ground attack aircraft and Shackleton maritime patrol aircraft were used to bomb rebel positions in the Radfan until British forces withdrew in 1968.

The RAF had withdrawn completely from the Gulf by 1971 and departed Malta in 1979, leaving Akrotiri in Cyprus as the only British-controlled base in the Middle East region.

SOUTH ATLANTIC SHOWDOWN

By the late 1970s, Britain's defence commitments appeared to have settled into a stable pattern, with increasing orientation toward Europe and extensive defence cuts throughout all three services. However, on April 2, 1982, the longstanding Argentine claims to the British South Atlantic territories of the Falkland Islands prompted a full-scale, sea-borne invasion of territory. The British decision to recapture the islands was made later that day and within a week a substantial tri-service task force had set sail. RAF Hercules and VC10 aircraft formed an airbridge to Ascension Island, in mid-Atlantic,

ABOVE: One of the RAF Harrier GR3 aircraft that was modified at RAF Wittering to carry Sidewinder air-to-air missiles before being sent to the South Atlantic.

which served as one of the staging points for the fleet.

At 0423 hours on May 1, as the task force gathered off the Falklands, a Vulcan bomber piloted by Flight Lieutenant Martin Withers dropped 21 453-kg (1000-lb) bombs onto the Argentine-held airfield at Port Stanley. The 12-hour, 965-km (6800-mile) mission from Ascension Island is the longest in the history of air warfare. During the land campaign, which began on May 29, Vulcans armed with Shrike air-to-surface missiles were engaged in operations against radar sites, while Nimrod maritime patrol aircraft provided anti-submarine cover and surveillance support for the Royal Navy. To supplement the force of Fleet Air Arm Sea Harriers, 14 RAF Harrier GR.3s were shipped south from Ascension prior to the seaborne assault at San Carlos and carried out numerous attacks against Argentine positions for the duration of the war. Although 17 of the 18 RAF Chinook heavy-lift helicopters were lost on board the container ship Atlantic Conveyor, which was hit by an Exocet missile on May 25, the surviving aircraft made a vital contribution during the advance on Port Stanley, ferrying artillery and supplies to the front line alongside a number of Westland Wessexes. The Falkland Islands were successfully recaptured and the Argentines surrendered on June 14.

In the ensuing years, an airfield facility at Mount Pleasant was constructed, capable of handling large jet aircraft. The RAF currently has four Tornado F.3, 2 Chinook heavy-lift and 2 Sea King Search and Rescue helicopters, two VC10 and 1 Hercules transport aircraft stationed in the Falklands – by far the largest overseas detachment outside Germany.

CHAPTER 9

BOMBS OVER BABYLON

In early 1991, after an unprovoked attack by the Iraqi leader Saddam Hussein on the neighbouring state of Kuwait, the RAF was involved in the campaign by a UN coalition to rid the country of the invading forces.

For some senior Royal Air Force officers, the Iraqi invasion of Kuwait on August 2, 1990 had a ring of familiarity. In 1961 Iraq had threatened just such an attack, only to be dissuaded by the deployment of UN forces, which included RAF aircraft and personnel, to the region. Iraq's sovereign claims to

ABOVE: An RAF Puma HC 1 helicopter at Ras al Gar in Saudi Arabia. Nineteen of these aircraft were deployed to the Gulf in support of the ground forces, and like almost all RAF aircraft in theatre were given the "Desert Pink" camouflage paint scheme.

LEFT: Iraqi supply trucks in Kuwait burn after an attack by ground troops in conjunction with air forces.

Kuwaiti territory were not foregone in the ensuing years, and became increasingly vocal when, in 1979, Saddam Hussein of the Arab Ba'ath Socialist party ousted Major-General Ahmed Hassan al-Bakr, who had come to power in a military coup in 1968, and so became ruler of Iraq.

Between 1981 and 1989, the Iraqi armed forces were engaged in a bloody war against Iran and its fundamentalist Muslim government, which had seized power from Shah Reza Pahlavi in 1979. In this they were enthusiastically supported by the United States, which favoured the Shah. The Iran/Iraq conflict helped build a strong and experienced cadre within the Iraqi armed forces, which by mid-1990 was the most powerful in the Persian Gulf. By the summer of

LEFT: A Buccaneer takes on fuel from a Victor K Mk.2 tanker over the Arabian desert.

BELOW: Tornado F.3 ZE732 of No 5 Squadron, RAF, flew 16 sorties during the Gulf War.

On August 2, 1990, the first elements of a powerful Iraqi invasion force crossed the border into Kuwait. Opposed by forces only a fraction of their strength, the Iraqis gained complete control over the country in a matter of hours. In the following weeks, despite a United Nations resolution demanding a complete withdrawal of his troops, Saddam Hussein consolidated his position. An unprovoked act of aggression against an oil-producing country with powerful international friends was decidedly unwise, but Saddam Hussein perhaps underestimated the scale of the response.

Throughout the autumn, a US-led coalition of UN members deployed air and land forces to bases in Saudi Arabia, Bahrain, Turkey, Cyprus, Oman, United Arab Emirates and Diego Garcia, in British Indian Ocean Territory. Although US forces made up the overwhelming part of the coalition, 28 other countries including Britain, France, Canada and Saudi Arabia were involved. RAF units, including Tornado F.3 interceptor and GR.1 strike aircraft, Jaguar ground/attack aircraft, Nimrod maritime patrol aircraft, Victor and Tristar tankers, VC10 tankers and transports, Hercules transport aircraft, and Chinook and Puma heavy-lift helicopters, were moved with their support units to the Gulf during the build-up operation.

VICTOR K.2

The Victor originally formed apart of the V-bomber fleet but in 1973–5 Hawker Siddeley at Woodford converted 27 of the aircraft into three-point tankers. During the Gulf War, the Victor fleet provided invaluable service to the coalition, flying the Olive Track racetrack refuelling course from their base in Bahrain. All the Victor tankers have now been withdrawn from service and replaced by Super VC10s.

1990, the dictator Saddam had at least 1,000,000 soldiers, 4000 tanks and some 700 front-line combat aircraft, including the MiG-21 "Fishbed", -23 and -27 "Flogger", -25 "Foxbat", and -29 "Fulcrum" at his disposal.

OPERATION GRANBY

RAF units were concentrated at five main airfields for the duration of the RAF campaign, code-named Operation

ABOVE: A Nimrod from RAF Kinloss in Scotland sweeps the waters of the Gulf for Iraqi naval vessels.

Granby. These airfields, at Dahran, Riyadh, Tabuk in Saudi Arabia, Seed in Oman and Muharraq in Bahrain, were home to some 7000 RAF personnel for more than six months. By mid-August 1990, Tornado F.3s detached from squadrons in Britain and Germany were mounting 24-hour Combat Air Patrols from Dhahran on the Persian Gulf, to dissuade Saddam from attempting a strike south into Saudi Arabia.

To support the Tornados, the Service hastily assembled a flight of Jaguar fighter-bombers from RAF Coltishall in East Anglia, and a growing force of technicians, planners and catering staff. The deployment was achieved with impressive speed, helped in no small part by the efforts of Strike and Support Command units in Britain and abroad.

During the winter of 1990–91, despite powerful political pressure from his Arab neighbours and a UN deadline of January 15 for his withdrawal from Kuwait, it became increasingly apparent that Saddam Hussein had no intention of giving in. Coalition planners at Riyadh thus began planning an operation to drive Iraqi forces from the country. The importance of achieving air superiority over the battlefield as a prelude to the land operation was fully appreciated. Once this was achieved, air strikes against ground targets could begin, with the aim of "softening up" the entrenched Iraqi

TORNADOES IN THE GULF

During the Gulf War, the RAF operated three of the four Tornado variants it currently operates: the GR.1 strike/attack aircraft, the F.3 air defence variant and the GR.1A reconnaissance variant. Powered by twin Rolls-Royce engines, the Tornado has a maximum speed at low-level of over Mach 1 and is equipped with superb terrain-following radar.

forces, eliminating the feared Soviet-built S-8 "Scud" mobile missile systems, destroying the Iraqi air force on the ground and providing close air support for the coalition advance.

FIRST STRIKE

The attack began in the early hours of January 17, 1991. More than 2000 coalition aircraft, including Tornado F.3s, GR.1s and Jaguar GR.1s of the RAF, were involved. In the first wave were four Tornado GR.1s from Dhahran, as well as four Tornado GR.1s and four Jaguars from Muharraq. The main task of the GR.1 crews was to attack Iraqi airfields with the JP233 weapon, which is designed to render a runway inoperable and prevent repairs. Aside from the difficulties posed by airborne refuelling at night, the attacking aircraft had to run the gauntlet of a huge barrage of anti-aircraft fire

ABOVE: The Umm Gahr Army barracks complex in Kuwait, which was largely destroyed during the first night attacks.

over designated targets, which one pilot described as a "wall-to-wall incandescent white curtain of light".

The attacks continued through the daylight hours. Iraqi air force elements that had survived the initial strikes made no attempt to challenge the overwhelming air superiority of the coalition, and many of the F.3 pilots flying CAPs in support of the ground strikes felt frustrated to be out of the action. The elation of the first day gave way to sadness when a Tornado crew was lost to ground fire on the night of January 17–18. The deaths of these two popular aircrewmen were keenly felt, although casualties were lower than most conservative estimates at RAF HQ in Riyadh. Operations staff were fully aware that the flat desert terrain presented a great advantage to radar-controlled Iraqi defences.

PHASE TWO

During the second phase of the attack, the range of targets was broadened to capitalise on the disarray caused to Iraqi defences by the initial attacks. Two further Tornados were

LEFT: One of nine VC10 K Mk 2 tanker aircraft operated by No 101 Squadron, RAF, from Riyadh in Saudi Arabia duirng the Gulf conflict. The aircraft has two wingtip and one centreline refuelling points.

lost, although their crews successfully ejected and were captured. On January 21, tactics changed, as low-level JP233 missions gave way to medium-level daylight bombing using 1000 conventional weapons. Press speculation about this switch suggested that losses during low-level attacks were unacceptably high. In fact, the change to medium-level bombing was a pre-planned tactic designed to be implemented once air supremacy had been achieved. RAF personnel on the ground worked extremely hard during the first phase to ensure the success of the strikes, despite the continual threat of attacks by Iraqi Scud missiles. Dhahran became the focus for no less than 37 of these attacks during the course of the War. A real fear in the minds of the people on the ground was that Saddam would use Scud to deliver the chemical and nerve agents known to be in his arsenal.

The switch to higher altitude flying exposed the Tornado and Jaguar crews to greater risks from Iraqi surface-to-air missile batteries, and, although attacks were often accompanied by ECM aircraft and fighters equipped with anti-radar missiles, RAF losses continued. By January 22, five Tornados and four aircrew had been lost in seven days of fighting.

Reconnaissance by the six Tornado GR.1As deployed to the Gulf proved that the Iraqi forces had suffered far more substantial losses, but when two captured RAF aircrew, Flight Lieutenants John Nichol and Adrian Nichol, were paraded on Iraqi television, it was for many a poignant reminder of the ever- present dangers the RAF servicemen faced.

Over the waters of the Persian Gulf, the dangers were less readily apparent, but nonetheless could not be ignored. From mid-August 1990, Nimrod crews from RAF Kinloss and RAF St Mawgan had been engaged in providing support for the naval blockade on Iraq and, in conjunction with coalition strike aircraft, were instrumental in sinking a number of hostile vessels They carried out this task with utter professionalism, though without due recognition, for the duration of the campaign.

THE FLYING BANANA

It became clear that the switch to medium-level bombing was having a detrimental effect on bombing accuracy and an equally negative impact on the morale of Tornado crews, who found they were simply not hitting targets. With press reports of rising civilian casualties in Baghdad, the Iraqi capital, the calls for greater precision bombing became louder both within and outside the Service. US forces had trumpeted the effectiveness of laser-guided "smart" weapons after the success of the initial strikes, but the RAF Tornado aircraft did not possess the necessary targeting equipment for these weapons. As a result, a unit of ageing Buccaneer aircraft (known in the RAF as the Flying Banana) equipped with Pave Spike laser designators was sent to the Gulf on January 23. On operations, the Buccaneer crews flew alongside their fellow Tornado crews, "marking" targets with the Pave Spike equipment that were subsequently attacked with 453-kg (1000-lb) Paveway laser-guided bombs carried by the Tornados. Twelve Buccaneers were eventually deployed.

TIALD

On February 6, four Tornados equipped with Thermal Imaging And Laser Designation pods were sent to the Gulf – after a much accelerated development program – allowing some Tornado crews to operate independently. TIALD-equipped Tornado aircrew operated alongside the Buccaneer and Tornado teams, attacking Hardened Aircraft Shelters and strategic targets in Iraq during the latter phase of the air war. Iraqi forces were subjected to intense air attack throughout late

LEFT: An Iraqi Hardened Aircraft Shelter that was destroyed by precision guided bombs during the Desert Sabre air operations.

January and into the early weeks of February as coalition forces built up on the Saudi Arabian border with Iraq in preparation for invasion.

The initial thrust of this attack was made by armoured units, supported by infantry and aircraft, in the early hours of February 24. Support for these units was provided by Chinook and Puma aircraft. A lesser-known but equally vital part was played by RAF chemical and nerve agent detection units that crossed the border with the troops.

One of the most important aspects of Desert Storm (the code-name for the coalition operation) was to reduce the effectiveness of the defence network in Iraq and Kuwait. Elements of the Iraqi army, including the élite Republican Guard, had many months to prepare defensive positions for their armour, extensive minefields and entrenchments. In the event, these defences were less effective than detailed in some media reports.

The ground campaign lasted little more than 100 hours, speeded by the enormous weight of fire directed on Iraqi positions as the advance moved north. On February 26, with coalition troops closing on Kuwait City, Iraqi columns began a panic-stricken headlong retreat north along the road to Basra under intense aerial bombardment, which marked their passage with a trail of indiscriminate destruction. The smoking columns of burned-out vehicles littering "Hell's Highway"' became one of the most poignant images of the War for the RAF personnel who witnessed it. On February 28, Iraqi commanders, with their war machine in tatters, signed an unconditional peace agreement. As RAF prisoners-of-war were repatriated, so the RAF began the operation to return thousands of captured Iraqi soldiers.

For all its horrors, the Gulf War of 1991 was one of the most convincing and awesome displays of air power in history, in which the RAF played a significant role. Some

---

RAF DISPOSITIONS IN THE GULF WAR

Dahran	Riyadh
18 x Tornado F.3	7 x Hercules
13 x Tornado GR.1	9 x VC.10 K.2/3
6 x Tornado GR.1A	1 x Tristar KC.1
	1 x HS.125
Muharraq	
13 x Tornado GR.1	**Tabuk**
12 x Jaguar GR.1	19 x Tornado GR.1
12 x Buccaneer S.2	
7 X Victor K.2	**Field Locations**
	17 x Chinook HC.1
Seed	19 x Puma HC.1
2 x Nimrod MR.2	

---

important and costly lessons were learned from the campaign, not least the problems of employing tactics designed for the Central Front in a very different theatre. Since the War, the RAF has revised its low-level tactics.

POSTSCRIPT

One of the conditions of the surrender was that Iraq make available to UN inspectors full details of its banned weapons programmes . In the seven years after the War these inspectors have found increasing evidence that Iraq has continued to produce and store these weapons. Saddam Hussein has shown his willingness to use "weapons of mass destruction" on numerous occasions in the past, and his refusal to cooperate with the inspectors of the UN has become increasingly apparent. In winter 1998–9, this attitude prompted the US and British governments to order fresh air strikes against selected targets within Iraq. RAF Tornado aircraft on permanent detachment in Kuwait and Saudi Arabia since 1991 were involved. Tension between Iraq and allied forces remains high and further actions – and reactions – are likely.

BELOW: RAF Jaguar bombers taxi out on the tarmac at Riyadh, Saudi Arabia. Some of the pilots have not yet closed their canopies, because of the stifling heat in the cockpit.

CHAPTER 10
THE FUTURE

The Royal Air Force is currently undergoing a major restructuring programme in terms of equipment, command structure and training that it is hoped will allow it to remain an effective force for Britain's defence through the 21st century.

This brief history of the Royal Air Force has hopefully provided an insight into the great variety of challenges the RAF has risen to meet during both peace and war. In the past decade, political and military threats from the Eastern Bloc have diminished, resulting in large scale cuts in military expenditure. The Strategic Defence Review of 1998 proposed a number of reductions in RAF front-line strength. At

ABOVE: A virtual reality simulation of the Eurofighter Typhoon cockpit. The aircraft will begin to enter RAF service in 2004, and is built in conjunction with Germany, Italy and Spain.

LEFT: Eurofighter is designed to meet the requirements of the four partner countries, although it is optimised for the air superiority role. The Royal Air Froce will receive some 220 aircraft.

the time of writing, the RAF has 6 squadrons of strike/attack GR.1 Tornados (78 aircraft in total), six Tornado F.3 interceptor squadrons (plus one flight of four in the Falklands, totalling 82 aircraft), two squadrons of Tornado GR1A reconnaissance aircraft (26), three Harrier GR.7 (54) and two Jaguar GR1A/B (30) offensive support squadrons, one Jaguar GR1A/B reconnaissance squadron (14), one squadron of Nimrod R.1 (2) and one Canberra (9) reconnaissance squadron, three Nimrod maritime patrol squadrons (23), two Boeing E.3 Sentry airborne early warning squadrons (7) and two Sea King (12), and one Wessex (5) search and rescue squadrons.

During 1998/99 one Tornado F.3 squadron (No 29) and one GR.1 Tornado squadron (No 17) will disband, leaving 154 offensive support and strike/attack aircraft. Also on

RIGHT: A GR7 Harrier, Boscombe Down, with full weapons fit on diusplay: SNEB rockets, BL755 cluster bombs and Sidewinder air-to-air missiles.

BELOW: A Tornado F.3 ADV on the ground, RAF Leucars, Scotland. The ADV will continue to fly well into the 21st Century, until it is gradually replaced by the Typhoon.

strength are 63 support helicopters, 78 transport and tanker aircraft, 286 training aircraft, 92 aircraft in reserve with the Operational Conversion Units and 13 RAF Regiment squadrons. Compare this with the 22,000 aircraft of 1918, and it becomes clear that the modern RAF is in numerical terms a much leaner force.

FUTURE EQUIPMENT

To replace the current fleet of Tornado F.3 and GR 4 Tornado, the British government has committed to buy the Eurofighter Typhoon. Flight trials suggest that this aircraft offers impressive performance, which, coupled with the latest aircraft and systems technology, will ensure the RAF can meet and overcome future threats. The lifting capacity of the helicopter force will be increased by 70 percent with the delivery of 22 GKN Westland EH101 Merlin aircraft, while 25 of the ageing Lockheed Hercules transport fleet will be replaced with the new Hercules C130J model. In addition, the Nimrod fleet is being upgraded to MRA4 standard, which includes improved radar, engines and mission systems. The RAF currently has a requirement for a Future Large

Transport aircraft. At present, this requirement is likely to be filled by McDonnell Douglas C-17 Globemaster III aircraft. Finally, airfield defence capability will be greatly enhanced by the latest generation of the Rapier SAM system. In the long term, the RAF is exploring the range of options for its Future Aircraft requirement.

The RAF currently operates the BAe Hawk as its advanced trainer and no replacement for this very successful aircraft is envisaged for the next decade.

FUTURE ROLES

The RAF continues to play a central role in the defence the Britain. While the majority of its strength is committed to NATO, the Service will also continue to make a major contribution to Britain's international obligations. Outside domestic defence commitments the RAF finds itself with increasing responsibility for peace- keeping tasks, crisis management, and humanitarian and rescue operations. Two notable examples are policing the no-fly zones in Iraq and providing support for the peacekeeping force in Bosnia. Although we are some way off a united defence force, greater cross-service flexibility, cooperation and resourcing is to be expected in the 21st century. Three examples of this are Joint Force 2000, which proposes replacing Sea Harrier and Harrier with a common type, the tri-service Joint Rapid Reaction force, which will require the commitment of part of RAF heavy-lift aircraft and the Joint Helicopter Force. The Joint Elementary Flying Training School at RAF Barkston Heath and the Tri-Service Defence Helicopter Flying School at Shawbury have already been established.

However, one thing that will remain unchanged as the RAF adapts to the demands of the future is its one abiding asset – the professionalism, dedication and courage of its servicemen and women.

ABOVE: Tornado crew of No 617 (The Dambusters) Squadron. The main asset of the RAF in the future will be, as always, the high quality and professionalism of its personnel.

INDEX